PRASIE FOR

The Intimacy Dance

"Upbeat, relaxing . . . easy to read and full of common sense."　　　　　—Sheila Walsh, *Washington Blade*

"Compassionate advice . . . I hope Berzon sleeps well at night knowing how many gay people she has truly helped."　　　　　—Tom Steele, *New York Native*

"*The Intimacy Dance* will help you to get through that third year, or it might even get you there in the first place."　　　　　　　　　　　*—Genre*

"This book shines in its extended recognition not only of homosexual relationships in general but of *long-term* homosexual relationships."
　　　　　　　　　　　—Publishers Weekly

"Berzon continues to take a leading role in helping gay and lesbian couples establish more meaningful and long-lasting relationships. Anyone contemplating a serious relationship or already involved in one would likely benefit from her insights."
　　　　　　　　　　　—Library Journal

BETTY BERZON, PH.D., is a longtime psychotherapist and activist. She is the author of the gay and lesbian self-help classic *Permanent Partners: Building Gay and Lesbian Relationships That Last* and *Setting Them Straight: You Can Do Something about Bigotry and Homophobia in Your Life*, and the editor of *Positively Gay*. She lives and practices in Los Angeles.

Also by Betty Berzon

Permanent Partners
Positively Gay
Setting Them Straight

THE INTIMACY DANCE

A Guide to Long-Term
Success in Gay and
Lesbian Relationships

Betty Berzon, Ph.D.

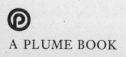

A PLUME BOOK

PLUME
Published by the Penguin Group
Penguin Putnam Inc., 375 Hudson Street, New York, New York 10014, U.S.A.
Penguin Books Ltd, 27 Wrights Lane, London W8 5TZ, England
Penguin Books Australia Ltd, Ringwood, Victoria, Australia
Penguin Books Canada Ltd, 10 Alcorn Avenue, Toronto, Ontario, Canada M4V 3B2
Penguin Books (N.Z.) Ltd, 182–190 Wairau Road, Auckland 10, New Zealand

Penguin Books Ltd, Registered Offices: Harmondsworth, Middlesex, England

Published by Plume, an imprint of Dutton Signet,
a member of Penguin Putnam Inc.
Previously published in a Dutton edition.

First Plume Printing, September, 1997
10 9 8 7 6 5 4 3 2 1

Quotation from a letter by Christopher Isherwood to Gore Vidal, by permission
of Don Bachardy.

Ⓟ REGISTERED TRADEMARK—MARCA REGISTRADA

The Library of Congress has catalogued the Dutton edition as follows:
Berzon, Betty.
    The intimacy dance : a guide to long-term success in gay and lesbian
    relationships / Betty Berzon.
        p.   cm.
    Includes bibliographical references.
    ISBN 0-525-94234-3 (hc.)
    ISBN 0-452-27747-7 (pbk.)
    1. Gay male couples—United States—Psychology.   2. Lesbian couples—
United States—Psychology.   3. Intimacy (Psychology)   4. Commitment
(Psychology)   I. Title.
HQ76.3.U5B467   1996
306.76'6—dc20
                                                                96–19392
                                                                   CIP

Printed in the United States of America
Original hardcover design by Jesse Cohen

As always, lovingly dedicated to the person
who is at the center of *my* life,
Teresa DeCrescenzo.

ACKNOWLEDGMENTS

To Terry, who continues to dance the
dance with me and who generously
allowed her privacy to be invaded as
I mined our own relationship to
produce parts of this book.

To dear friend Michael Shernoff, who
helped me better understand certain
issues regarding gay male sexuality and
the experience of loving a person with
AIDS.

To Dr. Brian Miller for providing me with
information and materials on domestic
violence.

To Don Bachardy for letting me use
Christopher Isherwood's quote and for
being such a sweet person.

To my clients for sharing their lives and
teaching me the lessons that I pass on
to you.

Certainly, under the present social setup, a homosexual relationship is more difficult to maintain than a heterosexual one . . . but doesn't that merely make it more of a challenge and therefore, in a sense, more humanly worthwhile? The success of such a relationship is revolutionary in the best sense of the word. And, because it demonstrates the power of human affection over fear and prejudice and taboo, it is actually beneficial to society as a whole—as all demonstrations of faith and courage must be: they raise our collective morale.

—Christopher Isherwood,
in a letter to Gore Vidal, 1948

CONTENTS

Introduction

Reading this book could be dangerous. It is designed to challenge complacency, to stir the pot, and to put courage to the test. If you are aware of problems in your relationship but you would rather not know what underlies them or get involved in exploring and resolving them, put this book down now.

If you think there is room for improvement in your life with your lover, you are committed to a permanent partnership (or aspire to one), and you are willing to be open to change, don't put this book down until you have read it, considered its ideas, and applied the relevant parts to your own relationship.

To illustrate what I mean by "dangerous," when I began to write this book I thought it would be easy going. I could call on two and a half decades of experience counseling gay and lesbian couples and, since the focus of the book is long-term issues, I could use my own twenty-two-year partnership for inspiration and ideas.

I thought about the kinds of problems my lover and I had dealt with through the years, what had precipitated conflict, and what we had done to resolve it. I went back over critical periods in our relationship, tough times that led to new understandings and better communication. The trouble is, the more I thought about this the more disconcerted I became.

I consider my partnership to be in good shape. I love, admire, and appreciate Terry. I'm certain she feels the same way about me. So what had I tapped into? Can just thinking about old dissatisfactions stir them up again? If this happened to me writing the book, what would happen to the people who read it? What was the lesson here?

I decided I'd better take some time off from writing to figure this out. The answers came fairly quickly. I realized that in tracing my way back through my relationship, I had stepped on a few emotional land mines I'd forgotten were there. Most relationships are mined with old hurts and resentments. We weave our way through the danger zones like dancers who have internalized the routine.

I believe my experience of unexpectedly running into old resentments is not unique. People do move around the minefields of their partnership, treading lightly to preserve the status quo. And then, boom! You step on a land mine you forgot was there because you have remapped the territory in the interest of peace-keeping.

The lesson here is one of awareness. The more aware you are of your own emotional underground the more likely you are to navigate the danger zones of your relationship safely. If there is covered-over conflict, you could put your foot in it at a time when it isn't in your best interests to do that. Maybe there are issues with your partner that need to be cleared up. Maybe an acknowledgment that differences are just that and nothing more is what is needed.

For instance, wouldn't life be much simpler if your lover wanted exactly what you want and felt precisely what you feel all the time? Wouldn't it all be easier if you didn't have those differences to cope with, no more frustration over who will get her or his way, no more grudging compromises?

How often have you wished you could transmit what you are feeling inside directly into your lover's brain? He or she just doesn't seem to get it. Words aren't doing the job. The message is lost. But, alas, we cannot *transmit* feelings, and we are stuck with using inadequate language to convey the abstract goings-on of our inner lives.

Because my lover is not me and I am not her, there are limits to what each of us can comprehend about the other. It is those limits that define the challenge of building compatibility. For some of us it is difficult to give up the desire to have a partner who is our mirror image. We keep trying to change the other person into us, which only produces tension and frustration. It takes relinquishing of that hopeless task for compatibility to succeed.

There is no *one* right way to be a couple, but there are some cautions to pay attention to, like not trying to change your partner into somebody else and not burying hurt and angry feelings that might later turn up as unexpected explosions.

In reading this book you may get in touch with some lingering dissatisfactions about your own relationship. You must then sort out what you want to do some work on and what you can accept and don't have to try to change about your partner or the life you share. That distinction is a crucial one.

I hope in these writings you will find some tools to help you make that distinction and work on whatever you want to improve. In particular, there is help with how to communicate your needs, understand when your child within affects your adult behavior, cope with change, and deal with the demands of increasing intimacy.

These are but a few of the "skills" I have found, personally and professionally, to be helpful in exploring what to do about whatever dissatisfactions with your partnership you might encounter.

WHAT IS A "LONG-TERM" RELATIONSHIP?

"So what *is* long-term?" I'm asked when I say this book is about long-term couple issues. Two elements are important to defining a relationship as long-term. The first is the assumption of permanence. The second is being with someone long enough to have shared a variety of formulative experiences—storms weathered, differences dealt with, commitment and collaboration established.

Research studies, my own work with couples, and discussions with other therapists produce the arbitrary but consensual conclusion that three years is about the time needed to achieve a solid and enduring relationship that can be called long-term.

Actually, I have heard from many gay and lesbian clients that this is the period of time they are "good for" in a relationship. After three years, they say, they get bored, or it's just too much work, or they have "fallen out of love." Maybe this "three-year myth" has become a self-fulfilling prophecy in our community. There are, however, some clues as to why three years might be a critical time to get past.

From their study of 156 male couples, Andrew Mattison and David McWhirter developed a theory about the stages male couples go through in their life together. They found that the third year of relationships tended to include the "decline of limerance" (being intensely in love), the highlighting of differences, and concerns with the emotional vulnerability of increasing intimacy. It is easy to see from this why some people misguidedly think that the relationship is going sour around the third year.

Surviving the third year, according to these authors, the couple moves into the next stage (the fourth and fifth years), which is mainly about *maintaining* the relationship. Several other studies, reported by Mattison and McWhirter (Sagir and Robbins, Bell and Weinberg), have found that male couples tend to break up around the latter part of the third year.

D. Merilee Clunis and G. Dorsey Green, in their book *Lesbian Couples*, have used Mattison and McWhirter's work in theorizing their own developmental model for lesbian relationships. While they do not assign specific years, they do describe the period *following* the second stage, "Romance," as "Conflict."

Insofar as any of these speculations are accurate, it does appear that the first few years for gay and lesbian couples are spent working out what the partnership will or won't be. So, for purposes of this book, more than three years defines long-term, which is not to say that couples in relationships of less than three years cannot profit from what is written here. Quite the opposite. There are many clues in this book relevant to getting past that magical three-year mark.

WHAT IS IN THIS BOOK?

INTIMACY

The increasing intimacy of long-term relationships is one of the rewards we seek in our love life. It also presents a dilemma. How close is too close, or not close enough? Why do some people push away the partners they love while claiming it is closeness they want most?

Much of this has to do with issues of control. Some people come to fear that the vulnerability to another that intimacy is about means they are losing control of their life. To maintain at least the illusion that they are still in control they *manage* how much emotional distance is allowed between them and their partner. I call this the "intimacy dance":

"We were so intimate last night. Why are we so far apart today?"

Or, just the opposite:

"We were so far apart and then suddenly we're so intimate!"

Understanding not only the rewards of intimacy but the peril it holds for certain people may help illuminate some of the darker corners of a relationship.

DISCOVERY

We look at discovery as an act of love—the need to know your partner better, which never ends, or shouldn't. It is ongoing dialogue that reveals the person's changing self—the shifting patterns of thoughts and feelings to be kept up with if you want to have a relationship that is current and alive.

Talking it over, asking questions, probing beyond the superficial are all ways to better understand this individual you have put at the center of your life. Materializing the ghosts of the past helps to deal with their influence on what is happening in the present. The unfinished business of childhood and past relationships sometimes complicates the simplest transactions between lovers. Discovery can uncover the plots and help clear up the mysteries.

MISSING SOMETHING?

Another kind of crisis that occurs in some long-term relationships involves an awakening to the passage of time and the concern by one or both partners that they might be missing something, especially if they became coupled at a young age. Boredom with the routineness, the loneliness of noncommunication, undealt-with tensions, change that is threatening—all of these can trigger thoughts of where the grass might be greener.

The fallacy is that getting rid of one's relationship will not guarantee youth revisited. The important thing is recognizing that this urge to flee the familiar may be a form of midlife crisis rather than a relationship failure. If, for instance, you missed the opportunity to sample a variety of romantic experiences before becoming coupled you may feel you have been deprived of the single life and its adventures.

My prescription is to address these feelings, preferably with your partner, and figure out what needs are involved here and what you can do to satisfy them short of turning your life inside out.

OUR CHILD WITHIN

Of course, we do not always behave so rationally as I am suggesting here. One of the reasons is that many of us have a child still within who emerges, often without notice, to wreak havoc with our adult reality. This kid is acting out dramas that belong to a time gone by.

The scared kid expects personal disaster, the needy kid hungers for love, the spoiled kid cannot compromise, the bad kid equates attention with love, and the mean kid is retaliating against past parental abuses.

I suggest talking to these errant children within. Denying or ignoring them can make them players in your love life at times when even *you* don't know what is motivating your behavior. Acknowledging them takes away their power to surprise you. Initiating a dialogue with them gives you a way to control their influence, integrate them more benignly into your sense of who you are. This is the balancing act we all have to accomplish in some degree—our child versus our adult, the wounds of the past versus the power of the present to heal.

TALKING IT OVER—DEALING WITH DIFFERENCES

"Can't you be like me?" is the lament I hear, spoken directly, more often suggested indirectly, from many men and women in intimate relationships. Some people feel invalidated when their partner does not have matching thoughts to theirs, similar feelings, or corresponding ideas on what to do about something.

Allowing your partner to be different from you is basic to relationship success. Sounds simplistic, but the inability, or unwillingness, to deal with a partner's differences is probably at the heart of much of the conflict in any couple's life.

What I call "constructive complaining" can keep conflicts aboveground, where they can be dealt with by negotiation. By constructive complaining I mean talking about dissatisfactions and saying what you want to change. In the best kind of situation talking it over leads to negotiation. Being open to negotiation and knowing how to do it well are prerequisites to a collaborative rather than a competitive partnership.

SEX

Sex is the stage on which many relationship dramas are played out, which is why it is so often a topic of concern. Monogamy versus nonmonogamy is an ongoing debate in the lives of many gay and lesbian couples. Enemies of desire, such as ritualized sex, substance abuse, and outside distractions can be intrusive visitors to a couple's sex life.

Dealing with HIV-related fears can present complications in the partners' sexual connection. If the couple is sero-different, it is important to talk about that, to give yourself permission to have and express any and all feelings about it. This is one instance in which clear and honest communication can keep an enjoyable sex life going as opposed to shut down over undealt-with fears.

The "other voice of sex" deserves to be heard also. Some couples' choice to forgo genital sex in their relationships has nothing to do with HIV or any sexual pathology. There are other possibilities for the expression of physical love. If this is what *both* partners want, it should always be an option and no one's business but their own.

DOES THIS HAVE TO BE SO MUCH WORK?

Between the various illusions around about what a relationship should be and the imperfect partners we *all* are, yes, there is always going to be some work to do. People who decide they are in the wrong relationship because they don't like something about their partner's habits, behavior, or approach to life are usually asking for a future of repeat performances.

You don't have to like the person you are with all the time. Most couples have lapses in the affection and admiration they feel for one another, but the *viability* of a relationship should not be in doubt because this happens. Over the years people change, and that in itself means work—adjusting, accommodating, integrating what is new. There is no avoiding work in a relationship that is growing.

THE YEARS BRING CHANGE

Turning points come from what is happening in the individual lives of the partners or in the relationship itself. The reordering of priorities may be necessitated by changes in one partner's career plans, income level, personal health, or the needs of biological family.

Some transitions, such as the emergence of violent behavior or substance abuse, can be so affecting that they threaten the future of the relationship if they are not dealt with. Suggestions for dealing with these turning points are made here. Knowing the resources available and being willing to make a plan of action are both essential to heading off potential disaster in these situations.

The changes a couple must make related to the advent of AIDS involve most aspects of the partners' life together. There are psychological and emotional issues beyond the physical illness and its demands—such as reinventing a sex life; reorganizing domestic duties; and being able to express fear, sadness, and anger without guilt.

THE OUTSIDE WORLD

The outside world forces its way into every intimate relationship. In some instances it is a positive influence—extended gay and lesbian family as a support system and involvement in the organized gay community. In others the effect of external events such as the breakup of couples in your friendship network may be threatening.

The families we did not choose can make demands that consume time and energy and sometimes put a burden on our ability to conduct our couple life as we would like. Gay and lesbian people in particular often have to work harder to establish good relationships in the in-law department, depending on how enlightened and accepting a given family is.

The needs of one's growing children can affect how open partners can be when being out as individuals, and as a couple, is desired. When your children get into their teen years, they may suffer special anxiety about having gay or lesbian parents, since social identity is so crucial an issue in adolescence. Your sexual orientation may not have been an issue before, and it may not be later on.

COUPLE COUNSELING

An important resource for gay and lesbian relationships is couple counseling, whether it comes at a time of stress because of misunderstandings and emotional hurts or is used as a preventive measure to build stability and clarity into the partnership as early as possible.

What the couple counselor does that helps is outlined here, as are the reasons people do or do not use therapy well. Guidelines are offered for finding a therapist, particularly what gay and lesbian people should look for in that search.

STABILITY, CONTINUITY, RENEWAL

Finally, stability and continuity are the rewards of permanency in relationships, and they are particularly important for gay and lesbian people creating family. One partner is the other's touchstone, and their commitment to each other becomes the base of strength from which they meet the challenges of their individual lives.

Integrating continuity with renewal insures that the spark will stay alive in our long-term relationships. Renewal may mean the resurrection of the language of love, lost through habit and familiarity, or it could be about recapturing the spirit of courtship or recommitting the relationship through ceremony and celebration. Paying tribute to our partnerships acknowledges their viability and strengthens our commitment to their long life.

WILL YOU FIND YOURSELF IN THIS BOOK?

Writing a book like this, meant for an audience of diverse gay and lesbian people, almost guarantees that no reader will find herself or himself on every page, or even in every chapter. What is typical of one kind of couple may be quite irrelevant, even alien, to another.

The questions "What am I missing?" and "Am I trapped in this relationship forever?" may hit the nail on the head for you as issues, or they could be thoughts you would never in a million years have. Dealing with aging parents may be what you are most concerned with right now, or it could be something you have not yet even considered as a possibility for yourself.

Are you concerned about too much merging with your partner—do you feel in danger of losing your individuality? Or is your issue *not enough* closeness, wanting to be more one with your lover? Obviously there is great variety in the kinds of problems gay and lesbian people deal with in keeping their partnerships working.

On the other hand, I encounter certain issues almost universally with couples—partners making unchecked-out assumptions about the other person, adjusting to change over the years, coping with the demands of the outside world. Sex—wanting it, having it, monogamous or not, if not with whom, when, how—continues to be of concern to many gay and lesbian couples.

I have tried to deal with a range of subjects here, knowing that not every one will be of interest to every reader. I also know that not all of you will agree with what I write on certain topics. Your experience may have taught you something different. When that is the case I trust you will take what seems helpful from my point of view and temper it with what you know to be relevant for you.

I have not tried to be comprehensive in this book. Some of you may be put off by what is missing—cultural diversity, for instance. Just as being gay or lesbian is the same and different from being heterosexual, what happens in multiethnic or biracial relationships is the same and different from what happens in partnerships that do not have that element. I have chosen here to focus on what is the same, though I am well aware that the differences can be extremely important.

Another concern I have involves the emphasis on problems in this book, but I don't know any way to avoid that. What happens in long-term relationships is always to some degree about resolving the problems that temporarily stand in the way of the pleasures of a partner-ship. Gay and lesbian relationships are not uniquely problematical. All intimate relationships are problemati-cal when they are not being fulfilling, fun, and loving.

Last, while you may encounter situations in these pages that have nothing to do with your life, the fact that they do have something to do with the lives of other gay and lesbian people would, I hope, earn your interest. In our community we need to understand each other bet-ter. We need to close the gaps—age, gender, politics, class, ethnicity—that prevent our touching each other's lives in more compassionate ways.

MY PERSONAL STORY

Throughout this book I have told my own stories—where I have faltered and recovered in my relationship, what I have learned from these experiences. I have in-serted my voice here because I want you to know that I do not write from a lofty place, knowing it all, immune to the real problems of maintaining love and commit-ment. I've been there. I know how hard it can be.

Personally, I have never been very interested in look-ing at other human beings with clinical objectivity. I am much more interested in the playing out of the plots and subplots that we all struggle through to have relation-ships that work and a life that counts.

We are not so different. I try to be a good partner and sometimes fail. I try to practice what I write, but don't always succeed. The important thing is that we try; we don't shut down, act out, give up, or move on. If there had to be one message from this book it would be that we *keep trying*. The best chance we have for success is from a place of commitment.

CHAPTER 1

The Intimacy Dance—
Its Rewards, Its Perils

The two men sat in my office week after week, fighting, glowering, hurling invectives at each other, and . . . holding hands! I was so fascinated by the seeming contradiction in their behavior that I sometimes forgot to listen to what they were saying, my mind stuck on the puzzling sight before me.

I soon realized that what I was seeing was a rather unique example of how two people managed the emotional distance between them. Fighting in the unproductive way they did created distance. Holding hands kept them closely in touch. The net effect was to keep the emotional distance between them relatively fixed.

In the years these two men had spent together they had evolved this way of controlling how close or distant they would be from one another. While they were disturbed by their frequent bouts, they resorted to them whenever their level of intimacy began to feel too intense to be comfortable; then distance was established, and they were back in a zone of comfort.

Human beings can be amazingly clever at finding unusual solutions to their problems, even though the solutions sometimes become more problematic than curative. The combatants in my office had become co-opted by their pattern. They were worn down by fighting, didn't understand why they did it, and wanted to stop.

My job was to help them see the connection between their growing intimacy, the fear it triggered in them, and the maladaptive way they had developed to deal with that fear. As they were able to understand this connection, they worked on gradually dismantling the pattern: moving closer, pushing away, rushing back, holding on, pushing away.

Once this acting-out pattern was out of the way, they could begin to deal with the real issue underlying it— why they were so afraid of increasing closeness and why they needed to manage the potential for intimacy so carefully. They came to see that the vulnerability associated with intimacy was the real threat—could they really trust each other to handle with care the most fragile parts of their beings? They weren't sure. They had to find out by talking about it a lot, which they did.

Trust evolved; they learned they could risk moving closer; they began to enjoy their closeness; they no longer needed to flee from it into combativeness. After that, whenever they fought it was cleaner. They didn't hold hands. When they did hold hands it was out of affection and simply wanting to touch the person they loved.

OUR NEED TO MANAGE

EMOTIONAL DISTANCE

Most of us have a need to exercise some control over how close we allow others to get to us at any given time. Often this is not even done consciously. We don't *plan* to have a fight with our lover today because last night the intimacy was so intense and passionate that it got a little scary. If this does happen, we are usually unaware of the connection between the two events—just another one of life's little mysteries.

"We were so close last night. How could we be so far apart today?"

I try to tune my clients into the rhythm of their moves: close, distant, close again. It is the "intimacy dance." In some version we all do the dance in our relationships. It is the poetry of movement that choreographs intimacy; the rhythms come from inside us and resonate to the inner rhythms of the other. We move in unison with a partner or in opposition to that person.

For instance, everything's going well, you bring up that predictable irritant—you didn't mean to, it just slipped out. Your partner dances away; now there is distance between you. You made it happen and you have to find a way to bring your lover back, but why did you have to push the person away in the first place?

Or there has been a disagreement with your partner and the chasm between you feels terrible. You want more than anything to be close again. You know the best way to handle this is to discuss what happened, but you are too impatient for that. You move toward your partner, talk sweetly, act a little coy perhaps, and make it clear that you are ready to patch it up. But you don't get the response you want, so you withdraw and become distant again.

You dance away and then dance back—wait, decide to talk it out, clear the air, and come to a new understanding of each other. Now closeness is welcome; it feels good. You move and your partner moves with you. It is intimate again.

The concept of managing emotional distance may seem a little abstract. This is not a distance you can see or measure, but the concept can bring clarity to a sometimes confusing sequence of events.

"Oh, I see. I always wondered why we so often have sex after a fight. It closes the gap between us. We're lovers again."

"But do you also see why you sometimes do just the opposite—have a fight after you have sex?"

"That's harder to understand. I guess it pushes us apart. It kind of breaks the connection we made sexually. We're on familiar ground again, not so vulnerable to each other."

"Being vulnerable is not something you want to be."

"Well, no, that's how you get hurt."

TOLERANCE FOR INTIMACY

Intimacy involves the ability to allow another close enough to know you without pretense, guardedness, or restraint. It can be wonderfully affirming—*and* a perilous gamble. You open yourself to another. You let your defenses down. You may be hurt, purposely or inadvertently. You are exposed to the vagaries of the human conscience. Anything can happen.

On the other hand, intimacy can be the greatest gift of a relationship—the person you know and can trust is there to comfort and protect and love you, no matter what. Intimacy brings out our softness, opens us to discovery, and awakens desire. Even as we feel the threat of it we experience its sweetness.

To deal with this dichotomy, we must learn to balance the fear of betrayal with the wish to surrender, not always an easy task, which is why tolerance for intimacy is so varied among people, even inconsistent at times for any given individual. Today I am totally available to you, tomorrow I may be defending against that closeness.

Our tolerance for intimacy is greatly influenced by what happened with our earliest caregivers. If that experience included freely given love, attention, physical contact, and validation, intimacy will be not be a problem for the adult. If love was uneven, attention sparse, contact withheld, and worth not affirmed, this adult will approach intimacy with caution.

In the best of all worlds families would be so enlightened and well adjusted that their children would always feel cherished, unafraid, and self-loving. But we don't live in the best of all worlds. We live in a society that offers almost no guidance for parenting, that values achievement over relationships and rewards conformity over individuality.

Most of us have had to deal with parenting by trial and error, mixed messages about love and sex, and confusion about who we are supposed to be. It is no wonder that some people come into adulthood needing to protect themselves from too much closeness, either because it is alien to them, and therefore threatening, or because intimacy is so mixed up with other complex feelings.

For people with this kind of history, the need to *manage* emotional distance in their own intimate partnerships can *seem* crucial to feeling safe and secure. What is essential here is that this be understood for what it is when it happens—not a rejection, not a sign of dwindling affection, but a need that one person has to feel in control of his or her own emotional landscape at a particular time.

The challenge is not to achieve the necessary distance from your partner in a destructive way—by starting fights or shutting down. The approach that will work best is probably the hardest—to put words to the feelings and say "I need to pull away right now. This is not about you. It's about me and the feeling I have of being more vulnerable than I can handle at the moment."

If you are a person who has difficulty tolerating closeness at times, you are not alone. Few of us are able to calibrate our emotional thermostat so accurately that we can always adjust to the highs and lows of a relationship. Where consistency fails us, however, the ability to speak up about what is happening can save a lot of wear and tear on the people involved.

Is this asking too much of a mere mortal—to always be able to identify your feelings, know what they are about, and articulate them correctly? Perhaps, but one thing I am sure of—we can all do better in this department, and the payoff is in the quality of intimacy we achieve.

TOO CLOSE, NOT CLOSE ENOUGH—

WHERE IS THE COMFORT LEVEL?

What is too close in an intimate relationship? What is not close enough? The answer has to be subjective, shaped by individual need, and influenced by the changing contours of two lives. Comfort level is a function of need plus circumstance.

You may want your partner to be closer, but the demands of the outside world make that very difficult or undealt-with conflicts are inhibiting a more intimate connection. You may feel that your relationship has too much closeness. You feel "merged" with your lover, lost in her or his identity. When this happens, you may need to reestablish your individual status.

NOT CLOSE ENOUGH

Sometimes we can feel quite lonely even in the midst of a loving relationship: "Yes, I know I have a devoted lover, but I feel lonely because she's not here enough/ he has his mind on his work so much/she is overwhelmed by the responsibility of elderly parents/he seems distant and preoccupied. I feel as if I'm always competing for my lover's attention."

As the years go by, one partner in a relationship might move into a more labor-intensive career aspect, be gone from home a lot, feel the burden of added responsibilities, or be motivated to do work at home in the time previously spent with a lover.

I have found that this can be a particular problem with male couples since men in this society are conditioned to put work at the center of their lives. Success in work is success in life. This is a difficult formula to contest. When I have worked with male couples in which one partner is distressed by having lost a lover to his career, I have encouraged the lover to consider a reordering of priorities so that there is more of a balance between work and home life.

A person clambering up the ladder of success doesn't want to hear that his or her partner feels anything but pride of association with such a high achiever. That individual certainly doesn't want to be told that there is something possibly more important than progress in a career.

Sometimes, when I am questioning priorities, I get a look that falls somewhere between disbelief at my naïveté and regret that I have taken leave of my hold on reality. What could be more important than success in one's work? To answer the question in a broader context, society refuses to give our partnerships the weight they deserve, so we should be making every possible effort to give them a high priority ourselves.

What might this mean? It could mean sorting through career-related choices and thinking about the effect a particular decision would have on your relationship. If your partner is unhappy playing second fiddle to your career, that is something to consider—assuming that in the worst case scenario the unhappiness could translate into your spending your future evenings auditioning for yet another Mr. or Ms. Right.

"Why do *I* have to make all the sacrifices? Why can't he or she just adjust?"

Maybe he or she can, but what must be conveyed in this negotiation is that the career builder cares about the partner's feelings and is willing to at least *look* for ways to compromise.

If you are the one feeling abandoned, it is in your best interest to put that on the table, even if you are a person who thinks it is self-serving and selfish to do so. Keeping silent about something you are so bothered by is very likely to create a subtext of resentment to your interaction with your partner.

Statements of dissatisfaction can be dealt with. Protests that run silent and deep under the surface of a relationship cannot be addressed or resolved. Intimacy suffers. The potential is for loneliness.

Indeed, career success can be most validating, but a relationship that works can also be a rich source of personal affirmation, especially if it is given the primacy it deserves. To love and be loved is your worth acknowledged—compensation earned that is just as real as the financial rewards that go with job success, more precious perhaps, even more critical to self-worth.

Another artifact of long-term relationships is the need that may arise for a partner to take on the care of elderly parents. This can be a demanding and time-consuming responsibility, so much so that the other partner may feel deprived even while understanding there may not be a choice. But is that always true, that there is no other choice?

I have been disturbed at times to hear that gay or lesbian people get the main share of caring for elderly parents because they "don't have a family of their own." It isn't true, of course, that we don't have families of our own—many of us have children. But whether we have children or not, fulfilling our partner's need for time and attention is just as important to the quality of *our* family life as meeting the needs of offspring is for our siblings.

I see this taking for granted that the childless gay person will be the parental caregiver as a form of homophobia, and I counsel people not to accept such an arrangement until they have thoroughly explored the possibility of sharing the job with their other siblings, if they are lucky enough to have some. It seems difficult for some gays and lesbians to give their own partnership the highest priority, especially when they're under pressure from family to take on the major responsibility for "the folks." I hear gay and lesbian people say, "After all, the demands of my life are not as important as the demands of my brothers' and sisters' lives because I don't have the responsibility of children."

Having children doesn't stop others from taking care of parents—others who do not have gay or lesbian siblings. I suggest posing the question "What would happen if the gay or lesbian family member didn't exist?" It is the assumption that gay people have no real family obligations that we must protest.

There are, of course, a myriad of additional reasons why someone might feel a partner is "not close enough." Organizational work in the gay and lesbian community can be very compelling. It can also become a serious competitor for a partner's time and attention. The same is true for recreational activities—tennis, softball, swimming, running, and so forth—that draw one partner and not the other.

Usually such conflicts are dealt with by negotiating compromises, but a workable solution is more difficult to come by when immersion in outside activities is being used to avoid problems in the relationships. How easy it is to fall into a pattern of not dealing with the dissatisfactions in our daily life, especially with a partner we've known so long and believe we understand so well. We give ourselves such inhibiting messages as "What's the use? This person won't care/won't change/won't get it. Don't make trouble."

When a couple comes to me talking about something so vague as "We're just not close enough," I ask for specifics.

- In what ways would you like to be closer?
- What intimate behaviors are missing for you?
- What would you like to see changed that would help you feel closer?

Such questions usually lead to an exploration of the issues underlying the absence of closeness. If you are feeling that you wish there was more closeness in your partnership, you might want to ask the questions above of yourself. In a sense, this is about the intimacy dance's being stalled, the rhythms for each partner so muted that neither can hear the other's beat.

Too Close — Where Did *I* Go?

One *possible* effect of long-term bonding in same-sex relationships is the loss of individuality that may be felt when two people seem to have merged into one. Since both partners are of the same gender, there is an essential alikeness that presumes compatibility.

Often the relationship is a welcome respite from the frustrations of living in a dominant culture that is hostile to gay and lesbian people. Partners may draw closer to shut out the world, becoming each other's safe haven.

In order to *maintain* compatibility and keep friction at a minimum, there may be a tendency to be as much like the other person as possible. Differences fall away. Mutual interests, attitudes, and styles evolve. The partners may begin to seem more like mirror images of each other than independent entities. The line—this is me; this is you—has blurred.

For some people this kind of merging is okay. They don't have to be so separate from their partner. They relish the closeness, love being with someone who is so much like them. When others perceive that the boundaries between them and their partners are disappearing, panic sets in.

"Where did *I* go?"

Nancy and Colleen

Nancy and Colleen came to my office with the complaint that, though they were very close, they were afraid they had fallen out of love. Nancy described her feeling that there was no "fresh air" in the relationship. Colleen said that she missed the passion of their early years together. Both agreed that they wanted to stay together but wanted more. More of what?

Over several months of sessions the question was answered. I heard the story of their life together. They spent all of their free time alone with each other. Though they'd had different interests when they met, they now liked all the same things. Since they were similar in size, they wore each other's clothes. They shared a vision of what they wanted their life to be as they grew older. As they talked, one would often finish the sentences of the other.

I thought that if I closed my eyes I would probably not know which one was talking, their voices were so alike. I thought of Nancy's early comment about there being no "fresh air" in the relationship. Reading my thoughts as I listened to them, I realized that the reaction I was having matched what their relationship had become: arid, stifling, constricting, and numbing. No wonder each felt no passion for the other. There was no other.

In order to feel love for someone there has to be a separate person—clear boundaries for where one stops and the other starts. Nancy and Colleen had become so close their identities had melded. I began to focus on the ways they had insulated themselves from the world, on how they had relinquished individual interests and activities. I slowly began talking about the importance of their having some separation in their lives.

At first they didn't want to hear what I was saying, resisting in all kinds of ways—disagreeing with me, changing the subject, missing sessions. Eventually, they were able to admit that they felt quite threatened by my comment that they needed to enable each other to be two separate people again.

My suggestions about how they might disentangle themselves were met with questions about why I wanted them to separate. I pointed out that I was not suggesting they separate but that they regain the boundaries that defined them as two different people. That might involve spending some time apart, pursuing independent interests, having social contacts outside the relationship.

Initially, Nancy and Colleen behaved as if they didn't know what I was talking about when I suggested that they pursue people and activities outside the relationship.

"Like what?" they would demand.

I began to be more specific: "How about one night a week you go out separately with friends?"

"Like who?" came the protest.

We went over people they had known but didn't see anymore, activities they'd once had an interest in but no longer pursued. We talked about the gay and lesbian community and the many opportunities for involvement that were available. That brought up a whole new issue.

Nancy said she felt threatened by the idea of Colleen's meeting other lesbians without her. It gradually emerged that one reason they had not been more socially active was because one (or both) at various times felt insecure about contact with lesbians, fearing that attraction to another woman might mean loss of the relationship. They had never talked about it directly, but doing so made it possible for them to give each other reassurances that they were together and both intended to stay that way.

It took Nancy and Colleen several more months to make the transition. Slowly, cautiously, they opened their relationship to friends and new activities, some even pursued individually. Soon they found they had much more to talk about when they were together. They were two separate people again. Intimacy returned to their relationship now that there was an "other" to desire.

Because women are socialized in this society to put a primary relationship at the center of their lives, lesbians tend to merge with their partners more often than gay men, who are conditioned to look to the outside world for their validation. While Nancy and Colleen's story is not necessarily typical of lesbian relationships, the potential for becoming enmeshed is there in all same-sex partnerships.

The healthiest relationships are those in which two distinct individuals allow—in fact, encourage—independent activity in a partner so that when they come back together it is with a certain excitement about sharing what has happened to them. It is the interplay of *two* lives that vitalizes the domestic drama.

A woman client told me recently that she and her partner decided not to go on an all-lesbian cruise because of all the predatory women they would encounter. Is it true that lesbians are inclined routinely to seduce one's partner away? I questioned that, but the anticipation of such a development was strong enough to keep these two women at home.

What needs to be explored here is the underlying fear that the relationship is so fragile that it is in jeopardy when they are in the company of other lesbians. This fear is not, and should not be, easily dismissed. It may reflect a troubling disbelief in the legitimacy of a same-sex union, or it may express a deep-seated insecurity about one's ability to love and be loved in an enduring way.

In either case, the need to avoid close association

with others of the same sex should be the subject of an honest discussion between partners to determine what the threat is. Quite possibly, it may be time for the partners to be more affirming of each other, clearer about their commitment to the relationship. Doubts about love and loyalty should not be silently harbored. They should have a voice: "Are we together?" "Do you love me?" "Can I count on your commitment?"

Many people have a problem with *asking* for love: "Well, if I have to ask, it isn't real and spontaneous. It's just an accommodation to me."

Match that with the people who have trouble *expressing* their love: "Why do I have to say 'I love you'? I wouldn't be here if I didn't love this person."

So we have people who won't ask and those who won't tell. If there are unspoken doubts about love everlasting, such doubts might make the bond seem more fragile than it is—something that *must* be protected from outside "predatory" influences. It is just this circumstance that sometimes results in a couple's isolating themselves and, in the process, becoming so close that they lose their separate identities.

INTIMACY ZONES

For some time I have struggled with finding a way to help people understand why they behave as they do with regard to the level of intimacy in their partnerships. If you think of relationships as emotional landscapes, you can go one step further and divide the landscape into distinct areas or zones. I believe couples settle into particular zones of comfort that then determine how intimate they will be with each other.

For the sake of discussion, I have envisioned the

landscape with four intimacy zones. Couples may start out in one zone and move forward or back from that level of intimacy as the years go by. I have named the zones: Safety, Conflict, Ambivalence, and Trust.

THE SAFETY ZONE

This is the kind of partnership that is characterized by great civility. The partners are polite, considerate, and minimally affectionate. Their relationship is orderly, having many routines that carry them through their days and nights. There are few if any surprises here. Many of the partners' transactions are ceremonious—stylized enactments of their devotion to one another. Both partners are satisfied with the way things are—controlled, predictable, unmarred by the unexpected.

Intimacy behavior in the Safety Zone ranges from contacts that are formal and devoid of emotional energy to contacts that are affectionate but at arm's length. Although the partners show great courtesy to each other, they do not get into feelings or anything that is deeply personal. Conversations stay on the surface unless there is a crisis, in which case they both go immediately into a problem-solving mode.

I have called this the Safety Zone because the controlled way in which these partners conduct themselves is designed to keep them on safe ground—no emotional eruptions, no attacks, no dealing with inner turmoil. Disagreements are glazed over, and there is a mutual willingness to move on from anything that might turn into conflict.

These are people who do not subscribe to the notion that the vital center of a relationship is in the playing out of feelings—quite the opposite, they want to stay away from that center because its draw is too powerful, too threatening to the tranquillity they depend upon to keep their lives together.

It is important to acknowledge that partners who live out their relationship in the Safety Zone are doing so in collaboration. There is no conflict about it. The arrangement meets the need of each person to live life as a constant, secure in the belief that they have matters under control—and that is exactly the way they want it. It is also the only way living in the Safety Zone can work.

THE CONFLICT ZONE

This relationship features movement back and forth between conflict and closeness. While it looks quite different from life in the Safety Zone, the same basic resistance to the draw of intense intimacy is at work.

There are resentments and tensions that seem to dominate the couple's interaction here, sometimes resulting in talk that one or both might possibly leave the relationship. Anger rides just beneath the surface of many discussions and is easily tapped into by a purposeful assault or even a careless remark.

Hostilities expressed cause the partners to draw apart, each cocooned in stubborn isolation, increasing the emotional distance between them. Or hostilities expressed result in prolonged discourse that goes around and around over familiar ground, never reaching resolution and, likewise, increasing the emotional distance between them. Learning about how to enlarge their relationship, a main benefit of *dealing with* conflict, happens minimally.

But that is never the whole story. When the animosity gets to a certain point it is as if a director shouted, "Cue the makeup!" The combatants stop and begin to repair their battered relationship. There is reconciliation.

Apologies are offered. The two move toward one another and contact is made affectionately or sexually or both.

They are back on track for the time being, but predictably there will again be a rift and the whole process will be set in motion once more. The end result is that there is never a permanent peace, only détente. There is also never uninterrupted closeness.

Intimacy behavior in the Conflict Zone ranges from contacts that are hostile and isolating to contacts that are conciliatory and affectionate. Usually both partners are dissatisfied with what is going on, but they cling to the pattern as though some centrifugal force were drawing them into it. Why? Because to let it go might mean moving into an intimacy zone that would involve increased vulnerability to one another and the challenge of integrating their lives even further.

THE AMBIVALENCE ZONE

In this relationship affection and closeness dominate—but not consistently. It is as though a warning bell goes off when intimacy becomes too intense. A monkey wrench is thrown into the action in the form of a comment that is hurtful or a misunderstanding that doesn't make sense. The partners are often mystified as to what happened. They were being so close, everything was fine, and then it all fell apart.

The episodes of anger do not last very long, and usually the issues are dealt with and provide guidance that allows something different to happen in the future (unlike what happens in the Conflict Zone). The partners here are willing to work on improving their relationship, though a painful process may be involved. Conflicts are talked through and often result in more closeness and trust, and intimacy is enhanced—until the next warning signal goes off.

Intimacy behavior in the Ambivalence Zone ranges from contacts that are born of conflict but are amenable to discussion to contacts that are loving and affirming. Why does the warning bell go off when intimacy is high? Because here, too, there is a fear of the unknown—What is involved in being closer? Will we be able to hold on to it, to hold on to each other? It seems easier to back off a bit.

THE TRUST ZONE

In this relationship closeness, openness, and trust dominate. There is spontaneous affection uninhibited by concerns about vulnerability, betrayal, or the challenges of unconditional loving. There are no significant barriers to stop the partners from exposing their feelings to one another. Personal experience is freely discussed without fear of judgment or ridicule.

While this relationship has its moments of conflict, and even painful exploration of issues, they do not create distance between the partners because they are not *designed* to do that. Conflicts arise, as they do in every relationship, but they are dealt with in a timely manner and are seen as expected and fixable rather than as something that threatens the quality, if not the foundation, of the partnership.

Intimacy behavior in the Trust Zone ranges from contacts that are about disagreements which are open to exploration and optimism regarding outcomes to contacts that are intimate without barriers, trusting without doubts, and loving without conditions. How does a couple get to the Trust Zone? Usually by working their way through the resistance to increased intimacy that is operative in the Safety, Conflict, and Ambivalence zones.

WHAT ABOUT YOU?

Of course, these distinctions among intimacy zones are not so clear-cut in life as I have suggested here, but they do describe the behavior of many couples I have worked with. I hope they also give some clues as to the emotional agendas that shape such behavior.

In which zone would you place your own relationship? Safety, Conflict, Ambivalence, Trust, or moving from one to another? Do you think your partner would agree with you? If you discover that you are not where you want to be, what do you think one or both of you can do to effect a difference? It takes uncommon honesty to introspect about these issues and perhaps even more courage to explore them with your partner.

HIGH-OCTANE RELATIONSHIPS—
INTIMACY OR AVOIDANCE OF IT

Once when my (Italian-bred) partner and I were in Rome, she decided she wanted to buy some luggage. We found a shop with a large selection. Terry settled on what she wanted, and she and the saleswoman began a conversation in Italian. Soon the discussion became heated, voices grew louder, hands flew through the air. The two women appeared to be in full combat mode. I couldn't imagine what they were so angry about.

As this was going on, my Midwestern sensibility was strained to the point where I felt the need to retreat to a corner of the store—of course, keeping an eye on my lover, who seemed possibly to be in dire peril. Then, as quickly as it had begun, it was over. The combatants parted. Terry returned to my side.

"What in the world were you fighting about?"

"Fighting?" she answered, surprised. "We weren't fighting. We were just discussing the price."

An Italian "discussion" can sound like World War III to the uneducated ear of a non-Italian. I once heard Cher in an interview talking about the first time she went to meet Sonny Bono's Italian family. She was shocked, she said, at the fight that broke out at the door, until she realized they were just saying hello.

The Italian passion for operatic bravura may turn the most benign transaction into a raucous encounter. But you don't have to be Italian to be drawn to passionate expression. Some people invest their relationships with a volatility that they find exciting even as those around them are appalled. Sometimes the excitement is a conscious experience. More often there is no awareness, the adversaries professing to hate their quarreling but feeling helpless to break out of the pattern.

Lars and Steven

Lars and Steven came to me complaining that there was no passion in their relationship: "We used to be so passionate and now, nothing. We just fight all the time." There followed a detailed description of their latest fights, complete with expletives not deleted, the smashing of breakables, and occasional hitting and shoving.

Steven, it appeared, was often the instigator of these fights, but Lars seemed always available to accept the challenge. They would fight over trivial things and over important things. They would fight in restaurants, at

parties, in the car, on the phone, and at home—
wherever they happened to be regardless of who else was
around.

Their friends were often distressed and embarrassed
by these altercations, but Steven and Lars didn't seem to
care about that. They said that when there was something to be ironed out they needed to do it on the spot.

On the second visit they fought in my office. As I
watched them I was impressed with the ferocity of their
exchanges, which didn't seem to go with what they were
fighting about: what movie to see on the weekend.
Steven accused Lars of wanting to see only "pablum
movies" that were devoid of any of the real drama of life.

Lars became furious. "You only want to see blood
and guts and rip-your-heart-out movies. How can you call
that entertainment? I go to the movies for recreation,
not to witness mayhem."

"The trouble with you is you don't want to face life,"
Steven said. "There is violence in life; there is heart-
break and tragedy. You can't just keep avoiding reality."

"Steven, you're just a sadist. You love to see people's
pain. I think you're sick!"

"No, Lars, you're the one who is sick, scared to death
of life. How did I end up with someone like you?"

And on and on they went, their voices growing
louder, their language more graphic, their bodies tense
as though poised for attack.

And then, I got it. This *was* their passionate connection—the fights carried the burden of their emotionality.
They engaged one another with a ferocious energy.
Whatever passion passed between them was embedded
in the scripts of those fights. It was as if they first *had* to
disagree; that was the foreplay. Then came the main
event, the fight itself. How passionate those fights were.

This was a high-octane relationship, combustible to the touch, anything but passionless.

When there was a lull in the battle, I made my interpretation about the nature of their passionate connection. Both partners immediately rejected my idea. Hadn't they told me that they didn't like their fighting? Why was I suggesting that they purposely created conflict, that they even enjoyed their combative relationship?

Okay. I next asked, "What would your relationship be like if you didn't fight so much?"

Lars and Steven looked at each other. They both laughed. Lars said, "It would be wonderful. We'd probably trust each other more. We'd be closer."

Steven agreed. "We'd probably be more intimate."

I carefully asked the next question: "What do you think you might be avoiding with your fights?"

The two young men looked blank. I rephrased the question: "What is missing in your relationship now?"

Lars sighed. "The intimacy, the closeness, the trust."

"Maybe," I suggested, "that's what is being avoided."

"Why would we avoid those things? That's what we want."

"But you say that without fighting that's what you would have."

And that is the conclusion they eventually came to. Lars and Steven collaborated, through their fights, to manage the emotional distance between them. While their fights were indeed passionate, they didn't produce closeness or intimacy, the usual by-products of passionate loving.

What is being avoided in relationships that are consistently and disturbingly volatile? That question is key to understanding how to break into a pattern that has partners in despair over their acrimonious behavior but unable to do anything about it. Most often one finds that the people involved have an aversion, for some reason, to those aspects of relationship that involve tenderness, vulnerability, and giving up control.

The task is to explore why each of those conditions has the meaning it does to each person:

- What are your fears about giving up control?
- What is there about being tender, or being treated tenderly, that seems threatening to you?
- What are your areas of vulnerability that must be protected?

Partners whose life together has evolved into rounds of endless fighting might want to explore these questions. It could be difficult to do, but most people who are caught up in a pattern of constant conflict usually do not enjoy what they are doing and want to stop. It is worth the pain of digging into one's underlying agendas to accomplish that.

RISKING, TRUSTING, AND GIVING UP
CONTROL—THE ENDGAME OF INTIMACY

"I don't want to get hurt again!"

How often I have heard this given as the rationale for someone's opting out of dealing with the problems in a relationship. Avoiding confrontation means staying in control because you don't trust your partner enough to risk exposing your true feelings. But when you have been in a relationship with someone for a while, avoid-

ing risk becomes more and more difficult. If you reserve
your trust and cling to control, intimacy will be elusive.

True intimacy occurs when you are willing to risk being vulnerable and you can relax your need for control
because you trust the motives of your beloved. True intimacy means being with another without the self-
protective strategies you may have employed in the past.

"What does that *mean*?" you might wonder. "Trust,
risk, relinquish control? That sounds my alarms."

And so it is for many people who feel they will be im-
periled if they make themselves *that* available to another
human being, even one whom they love. But this is the
endgame of intimacy—allowing another intimate access
in spite of whatever doubts you may have about being
hurt or betrayed.

True intimacy is about the willingness to make a fool
of yourself because you trust this person to know that
you are really no more flawed than he or she is. It is
about expressing your deepest fears because you can expect to be heard and taken seriously. It is about letting
your anger out because you know you will not be abandoned for doing so.

Intimacy is about allowing yourself to be loved even
though you may not always love yourself. That is the real
test of your ability to be trusting and close, because you
are letting the other into the most vulnerable of places,
where you are without the protection of self-love. That is
when the perils and dilemmas give way to the rewards of
intimacy. That is when the risks pay off—when the odds
for success in relationship are greatest.

Discovery and Disclosure—
The Never-Ending Need to
Understand Each Other Better

"I didn't just meet you yesterday, you know!" That is one of my partner's favorite lines. After twenty-two years, she believes she knows me well. She does—and she doesn't. I am sometimes startled at how accurately she anticipates what I am going to say or do. At other times I am shocked at how little she understands about me.

What I don't usually think about (and should) is that she knows only those aspects of my being that I have revealed to her. Since she has a steel-trap mind she remembers everything, but since she is not a mind reader she does not remember what she's never been told.

Discovery is an act of love. One of the ways to keep a relationship lively and interesting is to treat your partner not only as an object of your love but also as an object of your curiosity. Who is this individual I have lived with for all these years? Is there anything more I can find

out about the essential person? Have there been significant changes since we first knew each other? Are there
secrets untold, dreams unrevealed, fears unexpressed?

Discovery is an act of love because it says "I care
about who you are, who you have been, who you want to
be. I open myself to you to listen and learn about you. I
cherish you, not just my fantasy of who you are, not just
who I need you to be, but who you really are to yourself."

That is a declaration of love that goes beyond the pro
forma recitation of "I love you," because it asks of both
an added measure of vulnerability to the other. Disclosing yourself is allowing the other access to what is going
on inside you. It is that willingness to put fear aside, to
relinquish the self-protective mode, to trust beyond
where you have trusted before. This is what creates and
reinforces the bond of the relationship.

MY PARTNER AS AN EXTENSION OF ME

How easy it is when two people have lived together
for some years to begin to think of this other person as
a mere extension of you. No need for discovery—you
know her or him as well as you know yourself. For a long
time I got away with treating my partner as if she were an
extension of me. I was oblivious to the fact that I was
doing something unfair and insensitive.

I have an office in our house. That's where I see clients and do my writing, so I am at home every day,
which means that I am the one who gets to deal with the
many little (and not so little) domestic dramas that running a three-dog household involves.

When something went wrong, I was the one to take
care of it, but then I couldn't wait until she got home
to regale her with the details of the problem. I didn't

exactly meet her at the front door with the disaster report. I usually waited until she was just *inside* the door.

Often I would be puzzled at her seeming indifference to my account of our latest misfortune. When I finally had the sense to ask about this, she explained that she had just come from a day full of problems, complaints, crises, and various other challenges to her wit and sanity. Being hit with yet more grief the minute she walked into her home was not something she had much enthusiasm for.

I heard her. I realized that I was treating her as an extension of myself. Of course she would want to hear what happened the instant she appeared. Of course she would be as upset as I was. Of course nothing else could be as important to her as what happened to me. And of course that would all be true if she *were* an extension of me, which she isn't.

I admit that I was startled to see the truth of something so fundamental. I learned the lesson. I haven't assailed her in that way again. I wait. I bind my anxiety (as they say in the psychiatric biz). I let her get settled and relax, have some dinner, and then I assail her.

TAKING YOUR PARTNER FOR GRANTED—

DISCOVER? DISCOVER WHAT?

Familiarity is one of the great perks of long-term relationships, but it has its downside. You know this person so well that you don't really have to check out your assumptions about what he or she is thinking, feeling, or wants to be doing. Of course, *you already know.*

For instance, you assume your beloved will be thrilled to go to Disneyland for her birthday since she had such a good time there ten years ago, on one of your first dates. You make the arrangements to surprise her and are in for a surprise yourself when you find out that she is horrified. She would rather do anything at this point in her life than stand in those lines and get lost in those crowds.

Or you think you are being a considerate partner when you spare your lover the boredom of going to your office holiday party—only to find out that he is furious at being left behind.

"Well, I just assumed . . ." is one of the phrases I hear most often in working with gay and lesbian couples who have been together for a while. "Well, I just assumed . . ." is usually followed by an angry "Well, don't just assume! I'm here! Ask me!"

We all want to be understood and appreciated for our complexities, and that includes the possibility that we might change our minds about what we like, or need, or wish to have happen to us. Sometimes partners get a fixed idea about what their loved one likes and wants and that becomes an unshakable conviction. The challenge here is to avoid fooling ourselves into thinking we know our partner so well we don't have to do reality checks. If we really want to be sure we are right about what this person is thinking or feeling in a given situation we have but one choice, *ask*.

TAKING STOCK

"Oh, Jim loves to do laundry. That's our arrangement. I cook. Jim does the laundry. We've always done it that way."

"And is Jim satisfied to go on being the launderer permanently?" I ask.

"I don't know. I suppose so. He seems to enjoy it."

"When did you ask him about it last?"

Silence.

Because gay and lesbian relationships do not have a readily available model for establishing the division of labor in the couple's life, how this gets arranged can take on a special significance. Has there been careful discussion about who does what, or has the arrangement just evolved based on practicality and the interests of the individuals involved?

It is easy to just continue the patterns that fell into place at the beginning of a relationship. Actually that may be fine, or it may not be. It could be that your partner hates, resents, or is at least annoyed by the expectation that he or she is going to keep on doing those same assigned (even self-assigned) tasks forever.

More important than how an arrangement came to be is the matter of how, or if, it is going to continue. People grow, conditions alter, needs change. Only through up-to-the-minute discovery and nothing-held-back disclosure can you really be certain that everyone is still satisfied with what they are doing.

Just what is the state of your union? How about a periodic checkup? You might ask yourselves if you need to change anything important in your life, such as:

- Arrangements for the division of labor
- Discarding or replacing of certain of your rituals
- The way affection gets expressed between you
- New or different friends
- Future plans

Or you might ask yourselves about the status quo of any aspect of your relationship. Periodic checkups, however you might wish to conduct them, can prevent troubling symptoms from developing.

FORGOING DISCOVERY AS SELF-PROTECTION

Partners do sometimes forgo discovery, either because they believe they have to acknowledge a partner's boundaries and respect his or her privacy or because they do not want to be seen as complainers. There's nothing wrong with respecting someone's boundaries until *your* life spills through those boundaries and you need clarification as to what is going on.

Withholding your feelings to protect your image as a noncomplainer can lead to disaster if you find yourself so preoccupied with your feelings of dissatisfaction that it overwhelms your ability to think rationally. Being determined not to give voice to your resentments puts you in a kind of solitary confinement. You are then in danger of talking only to yourself.

Of course, sometimes commenting on a partner's behavior can come across as something other than an effort to improve the quality of the relationship. If your partner feels innocent of the behavior described, he or she may feel unjustly accused and angry at you. If the person is not innocent of the behavior, he or she may feel guilty and angry at you. Few among us like being confronted about something we didn't do, or caught in something we did do.

Coping with a partner's anger, reasonable or not, is the price we sometimes must pay for honoring our feelings, reasonable or not. But there is only one way out of solitary confinement and that is to deal openly with what is going on inside of you.

There are a few pitfalls to watch out for when you find yourself in the middle of this kind of partner confrontation. First are the messages you give yourself. It is tempting to *tell yourself* what an insensitive, self-centered, deluded person you are talking to; that your partner is interested only in being defensive; and that the situation is hopeless.

Watch out for these messages. They might keep you from hearing what is being said, or they may give you the impetus to bolt or shut down. Aborting a discussion that has been difficult to start in the first place will only put the dicey issues on hold.

The second pitfall to avoid is slipping into delivering only "you" messages, so that the discussion turns into a focused attack on the other person. You have a much better chance of being heard and getting the change you want if you can stick to "I" messages.

Not: "You are just too insensitive to understand me."

But: "I need to feel that *I* really am understood."

When your partner feels under attack that feeling is what he or she will respond to, not the feelings or issues you are trying to deal with. Presumably you didn't set out to deliver a focused attack. You set out to try to work through some feelings that you are having. Watch out for the accusatory "you" messages. They usually signal your partner to mobilize against you rather than listen to you.

The third potential pitfall is the triggering of deeper, broader issues than you ever started out to address. Sometimes you just want to talk about specific feelings or behaviors or a particular situation, but suddenly the discussion opens up to more pervasive issues.

"You seem to have a need to feel bad about yourself. It's as if you are just looking for something to make you miserable."

"I am at a loss to know how to help you. I always get the feeling from you that nothing I do is the right thing."

"This is a way in which we are incompatible. I guess we just have to live with it, but it continues to anger me."

You may not be prepared for this turn of events. You didn't want to get into the profound cracks in your own picture of yourself or the flaws in the relationship itself. This pitfall is a function of opening up any heartfelt issue between partners. It is a fact of life that when two people are vulnerable to one another, and interdependent, there are going to be issues that have been stored, to be dealt with in the future.

What to do? Try not to lose sight of your original concern. Keep coming back to it. However, it is equally important not to ignore or trivialize what has been stirred up. It may be a balancing act—keep the focus on your initial concern and also deal with the broader issues that are now on the table.

You may come to feel that you are in over your head, but this discussion is probably happening because it needed to happen for you to understand one another better. Give yourself some credit. You can see this through, even if you feel as if you can't stand another minute of it. Stay. Don't bolt. Don't shut down. This is opportunity. This is how you build strength into the core of the relationship.

Is honest dialogue more painful than silent conjecture? Possibly, but dialogue, risky as it may feel, has much more potential for reaching resolution based on whatever the reality may be. Protecting your image or respecting the privacy of someone you feel injured by are two ways to put yourself into an emotional limbo. You have opted to be safe—and powerless.

DISPATCHES FROM THE PAST—

DISCOVERING THE GHOSTS

THOSE SPECTRAL PARENTS

As if it weren't enough to stay on top of what is going on in the present tense of our relationships, there are those ghosts of the past who come wandering through our lives, misguiding our actions, or stirring us to battle with phantoms.

"My God, I'm turning into my father!" a client exclaimed. He was distressed to see that he was behaving with his lover the same way that his father had behaved with his mother—domineering and critical. He hated that behavior of his father's, but he had internalized what he saw at an impressionable age and was replicating the drama in his own life.

Usually we select one parent over the other to identify with; most often we choose the one who seems stronger. Even if we reject that parent's way of being in a relationship, we may pick up his or her behaviors. My client was appalled that he was following in his father's footsteps. He quickly set about consciously trying to catch himself when the specter of his father turned up in his behavior toward his lover. He disclosed what he had learned to his partner so they could collaborate on effecting a change.

Or, in another scenario, your partner cries out, "What are we fighting about?" Often it isn't what you are fighting about but whom you are fighting with that is the problem. Your lover has just betrayed you in the same way one of your parents did, or so it seems. You fight back with a fury that is confusing because your partner doesn't know what he or she did to earn so much of your wrath.

If you understood it better, you could disclose that the ghost of your mother just materialized before your eyes when your partner laughed off a promise she or he didn't keep, just as your mother used to do. If your lover could go one step further and try to discover what is going on with you at the moment, she or he might obtain information that would help in knowing how to deal with you more effectively in the future.

Unfinished business with parents frequently haunts our intimate relationships, whether it is wanting to be like them to please them (at least the internalized "them"), fighting their domination, or playing out with a lover the anger you were never able to express directly to the parent who really did betray you.

It's a complex business to connect cause and effect in these matters, recognizing that you are still under the effect of emotions that belong to another period in your life, emotions you thought you had long since finished with. We all recast our dramas with new players when we reach adulthood. The problem is that we are not always able to clue these people in to the parts they are playing because we often don't have that information ourselves.

Following are the stories of four couples whose lives were impacted by the influence of ghostly parent figures and who were able to do something about it.

Bobby and Sam

Bobby and Sam had been together for five years. When they came to see me as a couple they were thinking of breaking up, though neither really wanted to do that. Most of the time their relationship was satisfying, but lately they were both feeling increasingly frustrated by the tension between them. Neither professed to understand why they had so much conflict over minor matters.

Bobby would say he wanted to go shopping for clothes. Sam would say, calmly, that he didn't feel like shopping but would go to the mall and visit the music store while Bobby shopped. Bobby would become furious. He would say something nasty to Sam and walk away. Sam would feel puzzled and hurt and eventually angry, and they wouldn't speak for the rest of the day. Sam felt he was being reasonable. Bobby felt Sam was being uncooperative just to punish him. This kind of thing had been going on for several years.

Listening, week after week, to the accounts of their encounters, it seemed that Sam was always the villain in the piece, either browbeating Bobby, criticizing him, or being unduly punishing. At least that was the way Bobby told it. However, something was wrong with this picture. Sam seemed to me to be a particularly gentle, reasonable person, who cared a lot about his lover. While Bobby consistently made Sam the bad guy, Sam consistently denied that he had said or done what he was being accused of.

Soon one thing came into sharper focus. The most salient feature of their encounters was Bobby's anger toward Sam even when Sam hadn't done anything he was being accused of. It was as if Bobby needed these opportunities to feel punished and to push back at this person who was victimizing him. I thought I heard echoes of an earlier life experience.

Enter Bobby's father, a man who was a stern disciplinarian and who used belittling criticism to keep his children in line. In order to reinforce with his children who was boss he tended to reject anything they said they wanted and demand instead adherence to his own agenda for them. Bobby had grown up with a gathering storm of anger toward his father, who made him feel that his needs were unimportant and whatever he wanted wouldn't happen.

Whenever Sam indicated that he wanted to do something other than what Bobby wanted to do, Bobby would feel that his needs were being dismissed, and his rage at his father would be triggered. Sam had become Bobby's villain—belittling and punishing him. Since Sam had no idea that Bobby's father had entered the picture at these times, he was confused about what was happening and frustrated by Bobby's treatment of him.

Once Bobby began talking about his father and the connections were made to what was going on between Sam and Bobby, things began to change. Sam would ask what was going on when Bobby became angry. Sam no longer just sat with his frustration. He insisted that Bobby open up about his feelings.

As a consequence of focusing on their pattern, Bobby was able to catch himself when he was about to unfairly make Sam the villain again. Sam was learning not to allow Bobby to become a victim. They were both better able to deal with the issue of the moment rather than surrendering to the drama of Bobby's unfinished business with his father. The tension in their relationship diminished; they were no longer thinking or talking about separation.

Laura and Melanie

Laura and Melanie were in the seventh year of their relationship, something Laura felt quite good about since she had not been able to keep a relationship together for very long before this. Melanie was a particularly stable, responsible, emotionally mature person who

enabled Laura to feel safe and secure in their life together. There was one exception to this. Laura had a
tendency to be inordinately jealous.

Time after time Laura had learned that her jealous
feelings were unfounded, that Melanie was a faithful
partner who was committed to monogamy. It didn't
seem to matter. Laura's jealous feelings ran rampant at
the slightest hint that Melanie might be interested in
other women. Melanie *was* interested in other women—
but as friends, as colleagues, and as interesting people to
get to know, not as potential lovers.

Early in their relationship Laura tended to act out
her jealousy in ways that made it unpleasant for her and
for her partner. Typically, Laura would berate Melanie
for something she had "done wrong" during the evening. Melanie was initially mystified about this since, in
her perception, she hadn't done anything wrong.

Eventually Melanie caught on. Laura wasn't really angry about some wrongdoing. She was punishing Melanie
for what she considered undue attention to another
woman. Melanie pushed discovery—she insisted that
Laura talk about what all this meant to her. Since this
drama was uncomfortable for Laura as well as for her
partner, Laura tried to comply. She talked about her
fears that she would lose Melanie, and eventually that
brought Laura to talk about her mother.

Laura's mother, out of her insecurity as a person and
a parent, resented the demands this child so consistently
made on her. Not knowing how to deal directly with her
own fears, Laura's mother subtly (and unconsciously)
conveyed the message that she would be just as happy if
she didn't have this child.

Laura's fear that she was going to be abandoned,
starting with her mother, became a long-playing theme
in all of her adult relationships. Since she got the mes-

sage as a child that she was unwanted, she imagined that message coming from all of the important people in her life, especially her lovers.

Surely these lovers would soon find someone better than she to be their partner. To Laura, every instance of a lover's paying attention to another woman meant she was auditioning her next partner. Laura would soon be abandoned for someone more desirable.

Armed with a clearer understanding of the dynamics of her partner's behavior, Melanie was able to help put Laura's jealousy—her fear of abandonment—in a healthier perspective. Laura learned to see the ghostly power of a rejecting mother for what it was.

Miles and Norman

Miles and Norman had been together for fifteen years. They came into therapy because they had grown apart, and both were disturbed by this. Miles kept repeating, like a mantra, that he wanted to be in the relationship but he also wanted to have more of a life of his own. Norman, who liked doing everything with Miles, was bewildered and hurt.

"What happened here?" he'd say. "We used to have such good times together. Now you don't want to do what I do. You just want to go off on your own. I don't get it!"

When questioned, Miles had difficulty saying just what he wanted to do apart from Norman. He would go quickly to the issue of how inhibiting Norman was— keeping him from doing things on his own.

"What things?" I would ask Miles.

"You know," he'd say, "just things on my own."

Miles saw Norman as controlling him and he felt

rebellious, but his rebellion consisted mainly of complaining about the short leash he felt Norman had him on. Norman, on the other hand, appeared to feel mainly hurt, deprived, and angry. He was shocked when he heard himself described as "controlling."

Going back over the history of this relationship, it seemed that Norman had been the one who took the lead in most situations, and that had been just fine with Miles, who was happy to go along—to have someone to go along with.

This "arrangement" worked well for many years. Then, suddenly (or so it seemed), Miles began asserting his need for independence. From that point on, Miles struggled to be in charge of his own life, and Norman battled to preserve something of their old camaraderie.

I was struck by what a complete flip-flop Miles had made in the way he regarded Norman. It was as if Norman had been the good father for many years and now he was the bad father. But why did Miles need to make Norman into his father at all?

The answer emerged as Norman and Miles talked about their early lives. Norman was an only child who got lots of attention from loving parents. Miles had two brothers who were both quite masculine-identified, loved athletics, and were often taken to sporting events by their father. Miles was left behind. He didn't like sports, preferring to read and listen to music at home.

While Miles was happy not to have to attend football and baseball games, which he hated, he did feel deprived because his father paid almost no attention to him. This was the sadness of his young life—though he talked to no one about it, because he didn't know what to say.

When Miles met Norman, he was drawn to Norman's inclination to take charge and to his rather protective attitude. What soon became apparent was that Miles had found his surrogate parent and he was no longer the disfavored son. That is what played out for many years, and it worked.

Then, as sons will do, Miles began to grow up. A part of "growing up" is separating from the parent. Miles was trying to do that, but reality intervened. Norman was not the wise, understanding father, he was the lover who was being abandoned, and he didn't like it.

Miles, embattled now, withdrew even more, blaming Norman for holding him back. Miles was actually able to say that he really wished Norman would just let him be on his own some of the time but still be there to love and protect him when he needed that—just what a good dad would do with a son who was developing independently. Miles was trying to resurrect his father as a good parent in the person of Norman. It didn't work.

Finally disgusted, Norman told Miles to go do what he wanted. The problem was, Miles didn't seem to know what he wanted. He tried a few sexual escapades but stopped himself by thinking about how unhappy Norman would be if he knew. Obviously Miles was using Norman as a brake on his own behavior because he was ambivalent about straying too far from the relationship. But then, of course, he blamed Norman for "controlling him."

The task for me became one of revealing this pattern and helping the two of them see how it was affecting their relationship. That meant that Norman had to be encouraged to discover what was really going on with Miles and Miles had to be willing to explore and disclose what he was experiencing.

As they did communicate, it became clear to Miles that Norman did not want to be the father who would make up for Miles's childhood deprivation. Nor did he want to be the father who kept Miles on the straight and narrow. He just wanted to be Miles's lover.

Miles began to look at Norman in a different way. He saw someone who was a take-charge person, who was protective out of love, and who wanted a relationship based on the contemporary reality of who they were to one another. Gradually Miles was able to remove himself from the fantasy of Norman as father/rescuer. He felt closer to Norman, no longer needing to push away from him, accepting him as lover again.

Helen and Sylvia

Helen and Sylvia had a good relationship. They had much in common. They enjoyed the same things. They liked and admired one another. And, most of the time, they were quite clear about wanting to spend the rest of their lives together. The instances in which they were not so clear occurred when there was a conflict that seemed to defy resolution.

It was always Helen's inclination to try to talk about what was happening, to attempt some solution through discussion. Sylvia was initially cooperative in these situations, but if there was not enough progress in a short time, she began to shut down and withdraw. This left Helen frustrated, and she would then push for Sylvia to stay with it, to participate, to respond.

The harder Helen pushed, the more withdrawn Sylvia became. Sometimes Helen got so angry she began shouting to get through to Sylvia. That was Sylvia's cue to remove herself abruptly from the scene, leaving Helen defeated and alone.

For some period after each of these aborted encounters, Helen and Sylvia spoke to each other in shorthand, saying as little as possible, showing no emotion. Eventually they tired of the chill and they would gradually warm up to one another again.

This was their pattern until Helen decided she couldn't stand the frustration anymore. She had to discover what this need of Sylvia's to flee from conflict was all about. At first Sylvia resisted Helen's questions, but when she realized how distressed her partner had become she agreed to talk.

It took Sylvia a while to get to her family. She was reluctant to get into it but she finally opened up. What Helen heard was that Sylvia had spent her childhood listening to her parents fight.

Actually, Helen already knew that Sylvia's parents were contentious and had a tumultuous relationship. What she had not understood was how profoundly Sylvia was affected by this, how she had wanted desperately to flee whenever her parents had one of their loud and heated arguments, often lying on her bed with pillows over her head to drown out the shouting.

Sylvia talked about the fears she'd had of her parents' hurting one another or getting so out of control that one might drive the other away. When they fought she felt endangered, as if her life would never be the same because something terrible was about to happen. Sylvia had not only felt terrified at these times, she had felt utterly powerless—a child's helplessness.

No one in Sylvia's family ever talked about these fights afterward—as though they had never happened. Sylvia grew up holding the secret of her fear inside. There was no one to tell about it. Sylvia was okay with her secret as long as she was alone, but when she became involved with Helen the fear was stirred again when they had their first disagreement. She could only think of fleeing.

Sylvia was able to tell Helen that whenever they argued she started to have those feelings again of being helpless and in danger. All she could think of at those times was getting away from the danger. Confronting her past in this way, disclosing it to Helen, Sylvia began to connect with the idea that she had the power to control her own destiny now. She wasn't dependent on those parents any longer and therefore how they behaved didn't matter.

Having all of this out in the open helped Helen to be sensitive to what was happening to Sylvia when they had an argument. She could remind Sylvia of the reality of their situation, that she was engaged with her lover, no mom and dad around, and the only real danger was in turning away from the effort to find resolution.

These stories may seem somewhat extreme, but I don't believe they are that uncommon. We are all flawed, and our parents are no different. Everything we are and do and feel does not necessarily always flow from the way we were parented, but how we behave in our intimate partnerships often does reflect what we learned in that first close and dependent relationship.

It would be folly to ignore the mark our experience of our parents has left on us. In the matter of understanding yourself and your partner better, there is buried treasure in the ground of your family history. Some people don't like this idea, preferring to think that their lives are products of who they are in the present and what they have made happen themselves.

"Blame, blame, why do we have to blame everything on our parents?" clients say to me.

It's not about blaming. It's about understanding why you avoid conflict or seek it out; why you have a hard time trusting your partner; why you are critical, nag, withdraw, become angry, create drama, need attention; or why you are the most kind, giving, trusting, lovable person around.

It's about solving those little mysteries of who you are, who he or she is, and why there are times when the behavior of either one of you is inexplicable. The clues are quite often in the stories of how it was in the family, stories that should be told and retold between partners seeking truths that can clarify what might otherwise seem unaccountable.

THE SIBLINGS WE COMPETE WITH

Of course, Mom and Dad were not the only players on the family scene. There are those siblings with whom you had to compete for love and attention. If you left the family fold not having grown out of the competing mode you may still be carrying on the competition with your lover, keeping track of your triumphs and defeats in life versus his or hers, being envious of anything your partner has that you don't have.

I have a sister ten years my junior who, as a child, was prettier, healthier, and easier to be around than I. Now I have a lover more than ten years my junior who is prettier, healthier, and easier to be around than I. It is not lost on me that I sometimes resent the attention my lover gets from people. In my more adult thinking, I know that she reaches out to people more than I do and that is a major reason they respond to her. In my less mature moments I simply resent her "popularity."

The point is to have the awareness to be able to make the distinction between whatever leftover business of childhood and family might be operating and the reality of our present-day life. It isn't always easy to make that distinction, especially if we have been embarrassed by our feelings of envy or jealousy and have kept them inside, hidden from the people we want to love us.

It is easier to separate past from present when the past is openly explored and negative thoughts about yourself do not become rooted in a personal mythology—the beliefs you have about yourself. Assuming that you are unlovable because your flawed parents did not know how to express love is a personal myth that can keep you from enjoying fully the gift of a loving adult relationship.

It is wise to examine your own personal mythology to see if there are self-negating ideas that might be influencing the way you relate to your partner. Do you find yourself surprised that someone could be so devoted to you? Do you fear that you will be abandoned no matter how hard you try to be a good partner? Can you trust your lover enough to talk about these things, to ask for love and support as you explore some dark corners?

EX-LOVERS

Many souls can wander through our relationships. Not only do parents and siblings make appearances, but the ghosts of ex-lovers occasionally turn up.

> "Jack loved to work in the garden. Our house was always a riot of flowers. *We* never had to go to a florist to buy flowers."
>
> "Louise was such a good traveler. *We* never had a problem being spontaneous about finding a place to stay."
>
> "Mark was a fabulous cook. He could just taste a dish and know how to reproduce it."
>
> "Susie always knew when I needed to be left alone."

Are you supposed to be getting a message from such statements? Is there something you should be doing that

you're not doing? Is your partner trying to wis
Or is she or he just reminiscing, thinking out
dulging in a bit of nostalgia? Whatever the m
summoning up these reminders of relationships past can
be disconcerting, and *that* is something to talk to your
partner about.

What can be even more subtle to deal with is what
appears to be the silent rebuke. For instance, you are not
mad about traveling, as your lover's previous partner
was. How do you know if your lover is trying to let you
know that this is not all right? Could it be the travel
magazines he or she leaves around the house? How
about the inordinate amount of time spent in conversation with friends about their trips?

Rather than speculating on the meanings of behavior, a well-placed question would be in order: "Do *you*
wish you were going there?"

One person I knew told me that she had always been
faithful to her lovers, but her last partner cheated on her
a lot. Now, in her present relationship, for the first time
she is cheating on her lover, and she thinks it is to get
back at her ex. If ever there was a reason to exorcise a
ghost, this one ranks way up there.

The unfaithful lover illustrates how influential a partner's unfinished business with the past can be, how important it is to discover any phantom presence that may
be operating in your relationship. Such a presence might
be quite benign, but I believe that the more information
you have about what is going on in your life the better
able you are to guide its path.

Intimacy grows in direct proportion to the level of
openness and honesty in any relationship.

DISCOVERY, DISCLOSURE — OF WHAT?

What am I asking for here? Is it disclosure of your deepest secrets, your innermost wounds, the flaws in feeling that cause you to act foolishly sometimes? No. I am simply suggesting that you consider sharing a greater part of your emotional inner life with the person who is at the center of your life.

Whether your partner is cast as a hero or a villain in your mind at any given moment, there may be much to be discovered by letting this person in on what is happening inside you. Will you be understood? Will you be cared about? Will you be fairly dealt with? If you don't provide the opportunity for any of this to happen, you may never get to know how deep the feeling between you can become.

CHAPTER 3

Is This Really It? Am I Missing Something Out There?

Suddenly questions cascade through the mind:

"Am I doing what I want to be doing?"
"Is my relationship working?"
"Is this the relationship I want to be in?"
"Should I make changes in my life?"
"What should I change?"

Who among us has not had these thoughts, however fleeting? Who has not wondered in moments of conflict or boredom if there was not someone else for us—someone less complicated, easier to be with, a relationship that was not so much work? If we could change partners with the seasons we would probably never get bored, but in my observation people who live on that edge are usually not very happy.

I hear midlife crisis statements most often from gay men and lesbians who have been in long-term relationships since they were very young. It's not necessarily that they are unhappy with their partners. It is more that they feel they are at a choice point in their lives, thinking about what they have missed and what else might be out there for them.

"Am I where I want to be in my life? Do I need to do anything different?" too often gets translated to "Do I want to stay in this relationship? Is there someone better for me somewhere?"

The fantasy is that a new partner might revitalize you, make you feel good about yourself, motivate you to achieve more, give you a new start in life. It is an appealing fantasy because it puts the responsibility for enhancing your life on someone else. A nice idea—but unrealistic.

Many people in midlife (anywhere from thirty to fifty and on) tend to start taking stock, looking at their options, wondering what they might be missing and what they ought to do about it. The cogent questions are:

"Who am I?"
"Who do I want to be?"
"Where do I want to be?"
"How do I get there?"

I have worked with numerous clients ready to forsake their partners because that seemed the easiest change to make in a life suddenly beset by questions about the rightness of the choices they have made. In truth, they are in a quest for identity that is larger than what their partnership is about. Untangling self-growth issues from relationship issues is the task here. "Who am I?" has to be about a great deal more than who I am *as a partner.*

If, indeed, you have been in the same relationship, or some relationship, since you were very young, you probably have had thoughts about what you've missed, how you could go about catching up on the youthful adventures you didn't have, what delights are out there waiting for your indulgence.

Maybe you have needed to experiment. Perhaps you've been able to do it all in your mind. But when you have explored sufficient lost-time opportunities, I hope you have ended up regaining your perspective and seeing your relationship as an asset to your personal growth rather than a liability.

Marty and Doug

Marty had "escaped"—he sat in my office breathing a sigh of relief that he had left his lover of eighteen years and no longer felt *trapped*. I asked Marty what had been so confining about his relationship that he had felt trapped by it. He said it was the things that curtailed his freedom to be an individual—always to be "Doug's lover" rather than just Marty, missing out on the fun of gay single life, always having to worry about Doug's feelings if he flirted with someone, just experiencing himself as desirable to others.

I asked Marty to reconstruct what had happened just before he made his "escape." He told the following story.

Marty and Doug had lived a quiet life, tending to their pets and fixing up the house they'd bought. They had a circle of friends with whom they traveled, played cards, and did potluck dinners. These men knew each other well and were like family. Marty loved his friends, but he was beginning to feel decidedly restless in his life.

On Marty's fortieth birthday his friends took him to a trendy gay restaurant to celebrate. Marty drank a lot of wine and proceeded to expand the perimeter of his celebration to include several hunky young men sitting at the bar. Soon the young men were sitting at the birthday table and Marty was arm in arm with one of them leading the singing of "Happy Birthday" to himself.

During this carrying on Marty avoided looking across the table at Doug. He didn't want to know what Doug's reaction was. He just wanted to indulge himself. If he had looked at Doug he would have seen a forced smile on an unmistakably angry face.

When the evening was over there was no conversation between Marty and Doug as they drove home. Doug wisely chose to postpone his comments until the morning, when he would have a sober partner to talk to. In the morning Marty again tried to avoid Doug, but Doug demanded to have a discussion.

"What was going on last night?" Doug asked.

Marty gave Doug a long look and said that was a silly question, that it should have been quite obvious what was going on: "I was having fun on my birthday."

"And what about your lover, who arranged the party for you in the first place? I was embarrassed at your behavior with those guys."

Marty sighed and told Doug that he was just too prudish and uptight.

"Why don't you loosen up and have some fun yourself?"

Doug answered, "My idea of having fun is to be with you and our friends, not to pick up strangers in a bar."

"Oh, really, Doug, you know I'm getting bored with this. You're just too intolerant of anything that isn't done your way. I want to have some fun in my life and that's what I'm going to start doing in spite of you."

This conversation escalated into a full-scale unconstructive fight, aborted when Marty precipitously left the house, noisily banging the door behind him. In the ensuing days, they moved around each other in strained silence. Then Marty went out one night, and when he returned it was with a decision.

Marty told Doug he needed to be on his own, that he'd been in this relationship since he was twenty and he felt he'd missed out on too much. He said he loved Doug and was satisfied with their life together, up to a point, but he felt too confined. He needed to go out and "be gay."

Marty reported to me that Doug told him he was being foolish, thinking he could recapture his youth, giving up a good life with someone who loved him to play in the bars. Doug said he wouldn't stop Marty, that he'd rather have him gone than feeling deprived and miserable and being blamed for it.

Over the next few months Marty did "play in the bars." He flirted and tricked and was delighted to learn that he *was* attractive to other men. When I asked him how he liked his new life he said that it was wonderful, that he felt like a kid again. That continued to be his sentiment until one day he came in looking strained. He said he'd been out three nights in a row and he was exhausted.

I asked Marty what he thought he had been trying to prove in his new life. He hesitated, then said, "I guess I'm trying prove that I'm still a young man."

"Why is that so important?"

Marty's face took on a pained look.

"I don't want to be old," he said simply. "Nobody wants you when you're old."

"Wants you for what?"

"Oh . . . fun and games, sex, I don't know. I don't know what I'm doing anymore."

"I guess you're trying to reinvent yourself."

"Yeah, I'm being the gay boy I didn't get to be."

Marty looked at me and said nothing for a long time. Then he said that he'd been thinking a lot about Doug. He missed him.

"So, what does that mean?"

"Well, I think it means . . . that the gay boy wants to grow up."

Marty had lived out his dream of being young again, a dream that took its intensity from the youth ethic of the gay male social world. But Marty woke up from the dream, glad to move off the merry-go-round—the erotic chase always leading one back to one's self.

After much discussion, Marty was able to regain the reality of his adult relationship with Doug. Ground rules had to be renegotiated, and a renewal of commitment was made. The connection between the two men held fast enough so they could move on together.

We have all had fantasies about what we think our lives will be. For gay and lesbian people, the anticipation of having a loving and enduring partnership is at the top of practically everybody's list of what they want. When you are finally in a relationship and the fantasy seems to falter, the inclination too often is to think of hitting the road. Flight seems easier than fight.

Then it is time to begin to sort out fantasy from reality: "Okay, so this is not my ideal relationship, not exactly what I had in mind for myself, but this is what I have, what I've made an investment in, someone I do love. I am going to stick around and work this out, no matter what it takes."

This is what I always hope to hear, even though it

may be true that one's dream partner doesn't quite match one's real-life spouse. People fall into relationships for a great variety of incredible reasons, least among them, usually, finding the person who is absolutely best suited to be their partner for life. What that means is that there is going to be work ahead—revising expectations, accommodating, adjusting, negotiating.

So, what do you do if you have thoughts of greener grass and making up for lost time by being unattached? The first thing I suggest is that you preview what your life would be like if you were not in your present relationship. Walk yourself through it. Where would you live? Who would you see? How would you spend your time? What would you miss about your life now?

My second suggestion is to talk to your partner about the feelings you are having. Yes, expressing ambivalence about your relationship may hurt the other person, it may bring you anger, you may feel guilty, but keep in mind that you are doing this for a *purpose*. You are recruiting your lover to help you get through this crisis.

By not shutting your lover out, by bringing him or her into your dilemma, you are honoring your partnership. You are not trapped in the relationship as it is because you have the power to change it into whatever you want it to be.

The question for the two of you to work on is "What needs to change *in the relationship* in order for you to address the concerns you have?"

Maybe you want your relationship to be more serious—less partying and social life and more quality time spent alone together. Maybe you want your relationship to be *less* serious—not so much processing of what goes on between you, having more fun together. Just getting out of some of the routines of your daily existence and experimenting with new activities could add another dimension to your life together.

ROUTINES: HOW THEY COMFORT, HOW THEY INHIBIT

We all need routines. Without them our lives would be chaos. We have responsibilities, schedules to keep, other people's needs to consider, our own sanity to preserve. Routines keep order, and we need a certain amount of that to make sense of our days. The problem arises when our routines begin to take over whole aspects of our lives.

While a set way of doing things does insure predictability, it can also cut off spontaneity. You don't have to think about this particular thing. You have done it the same way for so long. You know what to do. Why do it differently? Why think? Why feel? Why take a chance? And if there is enough of this going on in your relationship it would not be surprising if one or both of you has begun to feel the boredom of *too much* predictability.

Is this all there is—the routines of everyday life, the orderly march from one task or obligation to the next? Where is the spice? Where is the challenge? Where did the dream go? The routines have taken over. Could it be time for something new?

A useful exercise here might be to identify (write down, maybe) the routines of your relationship and think about what it would be like to abandon any of them and come at these situations in a totally new way. Reverse roles? Different sequence? Take some risks?

For instance, you know that on Friday night you go out to dinner and the movies, Saturday you clean house and shop, Saturday night you get stoned and have sex, Sunday you visit the folks, Sunday night you watch television and go to bed early. Doesn't sound so bad. But what if you want to have sex on Sunday without getting stoned, or you don't want to clean the house at all, or you want to skip the folks this weekend or this month or this year?

Is any of that permitted? How often have you talked yourself out of bringing up dissatisfaction with a routine?

"I shouldn't rock the boat."
"If it works, don't fix it."
"It doesn't really matter."

I'd feel better about this approach if I didn't know that many routines in the lives of couples have not been negotiated or even discussed. They have just evolved. Maybe they met the needs of both partners at one time, but do they still? How can you know unless you talk about it?

How routines develop is a particularly important issue for gay and lesbian couples because we don't have the traditional guidelines that opposite-gender couples have, such as:

He always drives the car.
She always cleans the house and cooks.
He always initiates sex.
She is the nurturer and caretaker of the relationship.

So now we have two men or two women in a relationship. Who drives? Who cleans? Who cooks? Who initiates sex? Who is the main nurturer? It's all up for grabs. I have seen many truly creative solutions to the problem of who does what. I have also seen many dissatisfied individuals who felt stuck in roles or routines they didn't design and don't want to be in.

As an interesting angle on how some routines develop in gay and lesbian partnerships, I like the notion that Andrew Mattison and David McWhirter present in their book *The Male Couple*. They say that in same-sex relationships, lacking the built-in complementarity of opposite-sex couples, we often effect something they call "learned incompetence."

The idea is that one partner becomes much *less* competent in an area where the other partner is much *more* competent, thus creating a de facto complementarity. Is this a conscious process? Not necessarily, but it's fascinating how often you can see it if you know what to look for. Once the "arrangement" is established it usually becomes routine.

Here's an example of learned incompetence from my own life. Early in our courtship I was the more successful, in-demand member of the couple. I was older, more worldly and experienced. There was, however, one thing my younger lover did extremely well. She was an excellent cook.

Well, I also cooked. Since I am sixteen years older than she is, I was giving dinner parties when she was in junior high school. I could certainly put a meal together competently. But, little by little, I began to defer to her in the kitchen until it became established that cooking was something she was very good at and I could barely manage to do at all. Without realizing it I had collaborated to the point of convincing myself that I really didn't know how to cook.

Now, over twenty years later, the issue is moot. There is no longer a need to establish an area of competence for her. She is a highly successful person, admired and in demand, but the routine persists: I am the novice in the kitchen; she is the expert. We complement each other in this way, and I have no objection since the kitchen was never the venue in which I planned to make my mark in the world.

If this "arrangement" wasn't okay I would not simply accept it. I would make noise about it, as I hope you will do if, in examining your relationship, you find there are routines you just no longer want to continue.

Alice and Joan

Alice and Joan came to me in the tenth year of their relationship. They weren't quite sure what they needed to deal with. They just knew that something in the relationship was not working. Alice said that she felt bored. When I asked her what she was bored with, she couldn't be specific. Joan, on the other hand, had no trouble with specifics.

"I am tired of hearing from Alice that she is bored. What does she want? We have a lovely home, friends, good jobs, families that support us—what else is there?" Joan began.

Alice stared at the floor.

Joan was exasperated. "I don't know what to do for her."

When I asked Alice to describe for me the way they spent their time together, she brightened to the task.

"Okay, here's how every day starts. We have breakfast and we both read the newspaper. There is no discussion except an occasional 'Hmm' or 'My my.' Mostly we sit in silence. After breakfast we dress and go to work, a peck on the cheek is our leavetaking. When we come home at night, a hug is our greeting. After dinner Joan spends a fair amount of time talking on the telephone."

"To whom?" I asked.

"Family and friends."

"And what do you do while she's talking?"

"I watch television and do crossword puzzles."

"Every night?"

"Every night."

"What would you rather be doing?"

"Anything *with* her. I suggest going out for a drive, a walk, to a movie. No, she says, 'Let's just stay home and relax.' "

"What happens on the weekends?"

"Oh, that's easy because it's the same every weekend. Saturday morning Joan gardens and I sleep in. Saturday afternoon we shop for food. Saturday night we play bridge with friends, the same friends every week."

"And Sunday?"

"We read the Sunday paper, then we clean the house. We have an early dinner, watch television, and go to bed."

"Every Sunday?"

"Every Sunday."

Joan could hardly contain her impatience. "Now, will you tell me what's wrong with that life? It's peaceful. It's calm. It keeps us out of trouble. Where is the problem?"

I asked Alice what was missing in her life with Joan. She took a deep breath and said, "Excitement."

Joan stared at Alice. "Excitement? What in the world does that mean? You want to go on a safari or something? How about taking up parachute jumping?"

Alice looked at me. "You see? When I try to talk about this she makes fun of me. It's hopeless. I feel trapped. At this point I just clam up."

I asked Alice to say more about what she meant by "excitement."

"I don't want to go on a safari or jump out of an airplane. I just can't stand the sameness of our days and weeks. I'd like to be surprised, do the unexpected, have new experiences. That's what I mean by excitement. I feel as if I'm under house arrest."

"Sounds like you're angry," I observed.

"Bored," Alice said.

"No anger?"

"Okay, anger. Why does she have to talk on the telephone so much? *I'm* there. Am I not enough? Am I not interesting to talk to? I guess not. She doesn't talk to me at breakfast. I get a peck on the cheek in the morning and a hug at night. Can she spare it?"

"What would you like from her instead?"

"Passion."

Joan looked shocked. "Passion? We've been together ten years. We're old married folks."

"That's *the* problem. I don't want to be an old married folk. I want a lover. I need to be paid attention to, not treated as if I came with the house. I want you to *want* to be with me. I need to be more important to you than gardening or talking on the phone. I'm bored with all that. I want *you!*"

In subsequent sessions Alice and Joan began to look at the routines of their life, one by one, negotiating what changes might be made and how Alice's needs could be better integrated into how they spent their time. As for passion, Joan, taking it as a challenge to become Alice's "lover" again, found that she, too, welcomed a more intense involvement. Alice was no longer bored.

Most everyone feels boredom in a relationship at one time or another. That should be taken as a signal that there might be something brewing under the surface, something unexpressed that *needs attention*. I understand that opening up to the unknown can be a daunting prospect. We fear we may hear something that is painful, learn something we don't want to know. The alternative, however, is to put up with boredom and the chilling effect it can have on a relationship's vitality.

UNDEALT-WITH RESENTMENTS:

YOU DON'T HAVE TO BE RATIONAL

ALL THE TIME

Often I hear from clients something like "I can't talk about those feelings. I'd sound irrational!"

I say, "Feelings don't have to be rational to be real."

"My partner would just get mad if I said how I felt."

"So what?" I say. "That's not the end of the dialogue. It's the beginning."

Probably one of the greatest obstacles to working through dissatisfactions in an intimate relationship is the need to at least *sound* like a rational human being. Of course, *you* may be one of those people who have no inhibitions when it comes to being irrational, but this section is for those who are invested in appearing, as much as possible, to be sane, mature, and in control even when they are churning inside with hurt and angry feelings.

The problem is that rarely are we able to hide our feelings completely. They sneak out in covert ways that create confusion but don't allow an opportunity to clarify and deal with the issues involved. Does this exchange sound familiar?

"What's wrong?"
"Nothing's wrong."

"I know when something is bothering you. What is it?"
"It's nothing."
"Then why are you being so remote?"
"I didn't know I was."

It takes a lot of energy to suppress feelings, energy stolen from loving moments. It is as if the light goes out of a relationship when it is shadowed by unexpressed feelings. It becomes stalled until the need for a connection asserts itself again and one of the partners reaches out to the other.

Luke and Charles

Luke and Charles had been together five years when Luke came home one day to announce that his boss wanted to promote him to regional manager. Charles congratulated his lover and said that sounded great. Luke then said that the not-so-great part was that he would have to spend a lot of time on the road and be gone from home many nights.

Charles had a sinking feeling. He hated being alone in the house at night. The thought of Luke's not being there made him feel anxious. How could Luke agree to such a thing without consulting him? Charles was hurt, but he immediately began to give himself the message "Keep these feelings to yourself."

In the week that followed, Charles was quieter than usual. When Luke asked him what was wrong, he said that nothing was wrong, everything was fine. Luke knew that everything was not fine but he had too often had trouble getting through to Charles when he got into one of these moods. He backed off.

Meanwhile, Charles continued talking himself out of

his feelings. He told himself that this promotion meant a lot to Luke and he should be a supportive partner, that many people traveled in their jobs, that it was part of doing business, that it would have been absurd for Luke to turn down a promotion just because his lover didn't like to be alone at night.

It didn't work. Charles was still hurt, and he had worked up to being angry, but he didn't express these feelings to Luke. Charles had convinced himself that his anger was irrational and he had no right to be hurt. But in the process of suppressing his feelings, Charles had grown silent and sullen.

After a week of this Luke sat his lover down and insisted that they talk about what was going on. Charles tried again to say that everything was fine but Luke wasn't buying it. He persisted.

Reluctantly, Charles told Luke that he was having a hard time with the thought that he would have to spend many nights alone and that he was hurt and angry that Luke had made this decision without consulting him.

Luke said, "What decision?"

"To take the promotion and become regional manager," Charles answered.

"Who said I took it?"

Charles stared at Luke. "You did."

"No I didn't. I said my boss wanted me to take it."

"Well, did you take it?"

"No, I told him I'd think about it. I wanted to talk to you first but you've been so unavailable, I've been put off."

"I assumed it was a done deal, that you had decided and that was it."

"Well, you assumed wrong. If you had said how you were feeling at the time, I could have told you that I hadn't decided yet."

"I was afraid you'd get mad if I told you how I felt."

"Wrong again. Telling me *anything* you are feeling is better than being silent and sullen all week. When I ask you what's happening, you deny that anything is. Then I have nowhere to go. I began to wonder if I wanted to be in this relationship. I do, but I can't deal with you when you just hold your feelings in and pretend nothing is wrong."

I have seen a number of people like Charles who habitually tried to talk themselves out of feelings that they thought might displease the other person. Often these individuals are from families who convinced them, as children, that their feelings didn't count. They are so imprinted with this idea by the time they reach adulthood that they begin discounting *their own* feelings. As happened with Charles, such denial doesn't work—and it certainly doesn't benefit a relationship.

Unchecked-out assumptions, such as Charles made, are the enemy of open communication. They may promise an easy way out of dealing with conflict, but this doesn't work in the long term because whatever issues are involved don't make it to the negotiating table, where something constructive can happen.

Haven't we all had this conversation with ourselves: "No use starting a fight; it won't go anywhere. I probably shouldn't feel this way. I have to behave like a rational person even if I don't feel like one."

It is an act of faith in your relationship to *allow* yourself to be less than rational on occasion. After all, it gives your partner permission to do the same when the need arises—and it will, you can be sure.

LONELINESS

What we experience inside is ours alone. We can translate it for someone outside of us, but there is no real companionship in the inner experience. I remember a client who had AIDS. He was surrounded by people who loved him and cared deeply for him. His partner could not have been more attentive and giving, but my client told me, "I feel so alone."

When I asked him to say more about that feeling, he said, "No one can feel the pain inside me and the fear of what will happen next. No matter how many people are around me, I am alone with the pain and the fear."

Loneliness in the midst of people can be acute in the situation of illness, but it can also happen in the midst of a loving partnership.

In the beginnings of relationships the intensity of mutual attraction creates the impetus for involvement. Each person is at the center of the other's thoughts and feelings. There is plenty of attention, affection, and validation to give and to get. But then time goes by and the world intrudes. There are the distractions of career, social life, personal crises, family relations, the demands of everyday living. One's focus is broadened; the intensity of early encounters begins to abate.

For many people this is okay—a natural progression into the long-term phase of the partnership. For others the transition from intense limerance to a more moderated connection feels disastrous.

"We love each other but we're not *in love* anymore" is the refrain I hear from couples who think maybe they ought to break up because the "chemistry" is gone. Some partners describe a feeling of being abandoned when the intensity of limerance diminishes. What is lacking is a sense of perspective; what is suffered, I think, is a kind of loneliness, a shattering of the dream of unending, seamless companionship.

The truth is that when the emotional tone of the relationship shifts from the ardor of love's beginnings to the companionship of affectionate attachment the partnership is really just getting started, not getting ready to end.

There is another kind of loneliness that occurs when one partner becomes immersed in an activity outside the relationship and the other becomes too immobilized by the sense of loss to do anything but feel lonely.

Michael and Paul

Michael and Paul had been together three years. During the first two years the relationship still felt new to them and their focus on one another was just as intense as it had been during courtship. They were each eager to get home at night to be with the other. On weekends they were inseparable, doing their domestic chores, playing, making love.

In the third year of their partnership, something began to change. Michael, who was a writer, started a book project. As soon as he got home from his advertising agency job he would sit at his computer and work on his book until Paul got home. Usually Michael would stop writing then and he and Paul would start dinner together. As Michael got more deeply involved in his book, he spent more time at the computer, not stopping when Paul got home, leaving Paul to prepare dinner himself.

With the signing of a contract for the book, Michael felt pressured to meet deadlines. He started writing on weekends. Gone were the times of sharing household chores, playing, and lovemaking. Paul found himself alone a lot. He tried to occupy himself with various activities but he missed being with his lover. He didn't feel angry at Michael, who repeatedly told him how sorry he was about their not spending more time together, promising that it would be like old times when the book was finished. When they did spent time together Michael was quite loving and attentive.

After several months of this regimen, Paul began to feel a kind of withering around the edges of his affection for his partner. He was extremely lonely. He tried to tell himself that Michael loved him and that they were together and everything was fine, but that didn't help. He couldn't shake the feeling of sadness.

Little by little Paul withdrew into himself, always trying to put on a brave face for Michael but feeling disconnected from him. He became uncommunicative. Believing that he could not change the situation, he said nothing about it.

While Paul had been unable to express his feelings directly, the changes in his behavior spoke loudly of his unhappiness. Michael finally "heard" him and began a campaign to get Paul to open up about what was happening. In so doing he was again giving Paul the attention he had been missing.

As the connection between them was reestablished, Paul came out of himself and was able to speak about what he had been going through—the loneliness of losing the lover he had thought would always be the constant companion of their courtship.

When Michael and Paul talked, their old comfort with one another returned. They were soon able to set some new ground rules for their relationship—Paul to speak up if he began feeling deserted again, Michael to seek a better balance between his writing and time spent with his lover. Abandonment had been a false issue in the reality of their relationship, but the loneliness it produced in Paul was quite real.

Sometimes loneliness within a relationship is just about communication. Most of us need to be told fairly regularly that we are loved and appreciated. We need responsiveness from the person closest to us. Many people have a tendency to forgo intimate conversation after the first blush of love passes. The impulse to speak words of love may have waned, but the need to hear them does not go away.

One can come to feel very alone in a relationship that has all the accoutrements of the good life but is lacking its own presence. When discussions are about business as usual and rarely touch on the inner lives of the partners, one or both may begin to feel lonely—a loneliness that can subtly translate into the disillusionment of "is this all there is?"

THE WRONG SOLUTION: BAILING OUT

How tempting it is when your love boat begins to founder to think about bailing out, leaving it all behind—the problems, the work, the tension, the compromises. Get clear of it, be free of the constraints. Fly again on your own; experience the excitement of escape, new worlds to conquer, another chance at love.

There *is* a kind of universal impulse to run away from trouble. Everybody understands it. Everybody's done it. It's socially acceptable to check out of a *bad* situation. The problem is: what is a "bad situation"?

All intimate relationships are bad situations sometimes, so how do you know when they're bad enough to give up on? How do you match your investment in a life with someone against your dissatisfactions? What logic do you use to come up with the answer that tells you to stay or to go?

These are questions to plague the rational mind. Are there useful answers? I think so. For one thing, it's important to resist the temptation to survey your friends to see what they think you should do. It's fine to talk to a few people, but the crucial data for making such an important decision are inside of you.

I find there is sometimes as much support from friends for ending a relationship as there is for getting into one. But these friends do not have the investment in the relationship you do, or the memories of the good times, or the experience of the emotional bond.

If your friends are encouraging flight they'll tell you they will "be there for you," but they won't *feel* what you feel, or go through the doubts, the loneliness, the anguish. So, thank your friends for their concern and return to your own deliberations.

Another flaw that commonly shows up in decision making about breaking up is the idea that with a fresh start you won't have the same problems you are having in your present relationship. Just as we carry our virtues with us to subsequent relationships, we carry our faults, and it is a good bet that both will show up dramatically in the new venue. We don't get rid of our problems by getting rid of our partners.

THE RIGHT SOLUTION: FINDING OUT

The question should not be "What am I missing *out there*?" but "What am I missing *in here*?"

Looking outward for what is missing circumvents the search that is more relevant—looking within yourself to understand what is stirring and looking into your relationship for what seems to have been lost.

More questions to ask:

"Why do I feel this restlessness *now*?"
"What else is going on in my life that is troubling?"
"What could my partner be doing to make things better?"
"What could *I* be doing to make things better?"
"What do I want in my life that I don't have?"
"What is this really all about?"

These are questions that may not be easy to answer, but making the effort could mean the difference between misguided flight and the kind of self-understanding that enables wisdom.

Having the mind-set "I can get out of here any time I want" is freeing and offers the illusion that you are in control of your destiny. Having the mind-set "I am committed here and I do not have the option to leave" is binding and offers the opportunity to reap the rewards of permanency once you get past the fears of being trapped and of riding past the brass ring.

The Child Is Still Within Us

A prominent psychiatrist and personality theorist named Harry Stack Sullivan is said to have once pronounced: "We never grow up." I think he was right in that we never grow up *entirely*.

"Understand me, love me, take care of me" is the voice of the child that sometimes insists its way into our adult transactions, creating utter confusion since the appeal is usually not overt or direct and, to make sense, must be translated from the adult's behavior to the child's plea.

Much has been written about the concept of the child within, that vestige of our growing-up time that motivates us to exhibit behavior that is sometimes incomprehensible, especially in our close adult relationships.

The child is the vulnerable part of you that needs filter through, the part that looks to your partner with the hope that you will be competently cared for. Your kid may come in various incarnations, depending on what emotional history is being contended with.

The scared kid prevails when you anticipate disapproval. The needy kid is hungry and is frequently seeking emotional nourishment. The spoiled kid, being accustomed to always having his or her way, is the one who has a hard time compromising. The bad kid equates punishment with love and misbehaves to get attention. The mean kid is retaliating for the hurt caused by angry, denigrating parents.

All of these kids can make trouble for the adult whose interior life they occupy. They are like a hidden force introducing confusion in what should be the simplest of encounters. These are the kids who fear, yearn, demand, and rebel to get what they need. The problem is that they are hard to get at since their role in any given transaction is abstract.

In an effort to make the child within less abstract and more accessible, I have separated the scared, needy, spoiled, bad, and mean kids from one another. While these are not entirely mutually exclusive definitions, there is a tendency for one or the other kid to dominate in any particular person. I personally have a scared kid inside me.

THE SCARED KID

An overly critical parent creates the scared kid, who anticipates disapproval, punishment, or abandonment whether it's there or not. This kid is always looking for the ax to fall.

"You did what?"
"How could you be so stupid?"
"You're doing it wrong again."

These are the words that are imprinted on the scared kid's brain. They easily get projected onto a partner. Even though they haven't been spoken, they are "heard." There is a certainty that one's lover is angry or disapproving in a given instance because that is what the scared kid is used to. Expecting this kind of reaction acts as an illusionary shield against injury and enables the adult to be ready for the blow that will surely come.

The problem, as often as not, is that what is going on is an internal drama involving the scared kid and his or her internalized parent. One's contemporary partner becomes a stand-in for the player (parent), who may be absent from the stage now but is rarely far from consciousness.

Egged on by the scared kid, this adult misinterprets a lover's behavior as anger or disapproval, and there may then be a retaliatory withdrawal or counterattack. Now the lover, not having had the critical thoughts he or she is being accused of, is confused and hurt. The child has triumphed over the adult, the internal drama over reality.

My scared kid causes me at times to turn my lover into my critical mother. I withdraw, acting out my anger at her for rejecting me (which she isn't doing). The kid tells me that my lover doesn't really care about me. I am in danger of abandonment. I have to protect myself. I won't care about *her*. I'll close off.

This behavior makes her angry, and then I am *justified* in my need to protect myself from her. What a waste of time and energy. What a bind to put a partner in. How important it is to open up lines of communication with the child within to stop this drama from going too far.

I think there are a lot of scared kids inside gay and lesbian adults. Even if a parent was not overtly critical, what you knew about yourself that they didn't yet know had disapproval written all over it. One way to deal with this was to be the best little boy or girl in the world. That might have worked fine for the real child, but the inner child knew too much. It is not uncommon for the vulnerability of those early experiences to get woven into the adult relationships of gay and lesbian people.

If your scared kid is ingrained with the notion of being less than, not good enough, flawed in some significant way, you may be influenced by the child's self-doubts to convince yourself that you don't measure up as your lover's partner. It is especially important for us gay and lesbian people to try to tune in to our scared kids, to make sure that the early feelings of being different and "wrong" are not still operating under the surface to thwart our adult relationships.

Another way in which one's intimate relationships are affected by the child within is in an approach to life that is permeated by fears.

"I'm scared I won't get it done [or done on time]."
"I'm afraid to get into my feelings. I'll be overwhelmed."
"I don't want to get involved. I'm afraid I'll be hurt."
"I'm anxious. I don't know what it's about."
"I'm scared to try. I'm afraid I'll fail."

Living with a person dealing with these fears can be a challenge. You may inadvertently become the protector and caretaker, but in so doing you could be empowering the scared kid to be even more in control. Instead, the power of this child within should be defused by rejecting

"I'm afraid" as an excuse for not trying or for staying uninvolved.

Billy and Hank

Billy and Hank had lived together for six years. Hank was a little older and had a job that produced more income than Billy's. The pattern that had developed between them was that Billy needed help with a lot of things and Hank was the designated helper.

Billy would try to fix something around the house and then have a problem with it. Hank would come along and say, "Here, let me do that."

Billy was only too glad to turn the job over to Hank because he had not wanted to start it in the first place, afraid that he wouldn't do it right. That part of Billy's insecurity didn't bother Hank—or Billy. What *was* troublesome was when Billy came to the conclusion periodically that Hank disapproved of him and was thinking of leaving the relationship. None of this was true.

Hank liked being the rescuer and the strong one. What he didn't like was the "wounded" Billy, who would withdraw and pout as a defense against angry and disapproving feelings he incorrectly attributed to Hank. Billy had a scared kid inside him who expected to be chastised, punished, or worse, abandoned.

Billy's father had been a harsh taskmaster, frequently criticizing his son, giving Billy the feeling that he couldn't do anything right. Actually, Billy's father was trying to mold his son to be more the manly little boy he desired him to be. It was simply not in Billy's nature to excel at the things his father pushed him into, so he ended up feeling inadequate and a disappointment to the man he wanted to love him.

Then Billy grew up and got together with Hank, who was strong like his father. Billy brought his feeling of inadequacy into the relationship, and eventually he began to believe that he was a disappointment to Hank, just as he had been to the other man he wanted to love him. That was when Billy would withdraw, angering Hank because he didn't know what he had done to deserve being shut out.

Billy's scared kid had a lot of power in the relationship. It kept Hank at arm's length and Billy stuck in his notion that Hank was another critical parent. Without knowing what he was doing, Hank challenged the kid. He did this by not letting Billy get away with withdrawing, by forcing him to talk about his feeling that he was inadequate and a disappointment to Hank, neither of which was true.

By focusing on the issue of Billy's expectations of disapproval, Billy was eventually able to separate Hank from his father. The scared kid got better integrated into Billy the adult so that a child-within takeover was much more difficult to accomplish. Billy's and Hank's partnership became more equitable, though Billy still needed help with a lot of things and Hank was only too glad to be the helper.

THE NEEDY KID

This is the one who has a large empty place inside, who is hungry for love and spends an inordinate amount of time seeking emotional nourishment. When the needy kid is in control, there isn't ever enough time being spent or attention being paid. Affirmation and reassurance are constantly being sought. The need for affection is like a bottomless pit.

Needy kids are produced by parents who did not provide the love and valuing necessary for their children to develop into fulfilled, self-appreciating adults. It is as though the mirror cracked—missing is that experience of looking into a parent's eyes and seeing reflected a cherished, admired, wholly accepted human being.

If there was love, it might have been complicated by parental inadequacy. Perhaps this parent was too self-absorbed to put out what was needed. Maybe he or she was too busy with other things—or simply lacked the necessary emotional skills. Possibly this parent's own parenting models were significantly flawed.

Whatever their origin, needy kids cause the adults they inhabit to have heady issues with the accessibility of their partners and how much affection is being tendered to them. It is almost as if a lover's job is to fill up the empty place inside. That demand can become so preoccupying that other relationship issues become obscured.

"I need more affection from you."

"I need to *hear* that you love me more often."

"I want to feel your touch. I know you love me, but my body needs to know it, too."

"I'd like to feel more appreciated by you."

"Will you love me forever, no matter what?"

These are not unreasonable requests, unless they become the mantras of a relationship, incantations that are constants in the partners' dialogue. "Like me." "Love me." "Touch me." "Value me." "Reassure me." "Heal me." The needy kid within can be very demanding. The adult must learn to be vigilant, to not let the kid take over and rule the relationship.

Kelsey and Carol

What attracted Kelsey to Carol in the first place was her self-sufficiency. She ran her own business, was active in the community, and had a plan for her life that seemed well thought out and sensible. When they decided to live together, it was Carol's condo Kelsey moved into because it was large and well located. Carol seemed to have her act together like few people Kelsey had known.

It was about six months into the relationship when things began to change. Carol began to complain that Kelsey didn't give her enough attention and didn't seem as committed to the relationship as she was. This came as a surprise to Kelsey, who felt very committed and thought she was being quite attentive to Carol.

Carol's complaints grew more insistent. Kelsey tried hard to be affectionate and loving whenever she was with Carol. Sometimes the problem would seem to disappear. Carol was her old self—confident, assertive, and independent. Then, suddenly, that person would be gone and there would be this needy child in her place, pleading for love and reassurance.

Kelsey was confused. It was almost as if she were in a relationship with two people. She started to notice what kinds of things preceded Carol's transformations, especially when the needy child emerged. Eventually she could see a pattern. When they had a disagreement, Carol would become anxious and begin tugging at Kelsey. She had to have immediate evidence that Kelsey still loved her.

It was as if their bond was a fragile thread that Kelsey was in charge of and that could be broken at any time, leaving Carol alone and loveless. It could take days for Carol to hear enough, be made love to enough, be reassured enough to return to her old self.

In many conversations over the years Kelsey came to understand the origins of Carol's dilemma—a mother who was alternately loving and rejecting, a woman who tried to be a good parent but found motherhood too much to cope with. Since Carol was the source of her mother's frustration, it was she who suffered—being alternately drawn in and embraced, then pushed away and rejected.

Carol had saved herself by leaving home to go to college and never returning again. She found other models for her life and learned to be a successful person in the world. What she'd never learned was how to contain the needy kid inside when she got into a relationship that seemed to resemble the intimate but tenuous bond she had to her mother.

Kelsey and Carol worked on this aspect of their relationship until it was no longer a source of confusion and conflict. Carol did learn to communicate with the needy child within, to gain control of that internal drama so that her loving relationship with Kelsey could have a life of its own.

THE BAD KID

Bad kids as adults are often disconcerting. They sabotage their own situations. They seem to be *asking* for punishment. Why do they do these things? It makes no sense. Everything is going along fine and then the person does something hurtful or destructive, creating wrath, inviting rejection.

It seems a mystery, but it isn't. The bad kid acted out a lot as a child because this turned out to be the main way he or she could get attention from a parent. Misbehavior was noticed. It got a response. So what if the response was a slap or a shout? It was attention. They knew you were there when you spilled the milk on purpose or knowingly tracked mud into the house.

For children, attention is love. For the bad kid, punishment is attention, and that is equated with love. For the adult with the bad kid inside, the way to get a response out of a loved one is to commit a punishable act. Does this make sense? It does to the child within. It doesn't to the partner, who must figure out why a lover is doing these incomprehensible things, making trouble so unnecessarily.

One has to wonder why so many children in our society must invent ways to get love. What has caused this disaffection of some parents from their own children? How does it come to be that certain children are not noticed until they break something—a rule, an object, an agreement, the law? For people like this self-sabotage can become a way of life.

What happens to the adult whose childhood was one long campaign to be acknowledged, even if it meant bearing the brunt of a parent's anger? In grown-up relations the bad kid is combat ready. If a partner becomes too busy with something else, watch out, trouble ahead.

The kid knows how to get your attention: mess up the plans, disappear for a day, threaten a breakup, betray an agreement. Ways to be hurtful and generate anger are countless. The bad kid is masterful at finding them. Now the partner is puzzled. Everything seemed to be going well until, inexplicably, there was this chaos. There has to be antagonism and a fight. What is going on here?

Once the trouble starts, the bad kid within can relax because the message has been delivered: "Pay attention to me. Acknowledge me. Your anger feels good. You know I'm here. I'm okay again."

Relationships like this can become a crucible in

which the unsuspecting partner is left in a state of confusion every time chaos is created for no apparent reason. The problem is that this partner is looking for explanations in *the couple's interaction* when it is the inner world of the other person that holds the clues.

Alan and Chris

Alan and Chris met at their local gay men's chorus. Both loved to sing and found in that activity a peaceful retreat from the worries of career and the agonies of friends' struggling with AIDS. Their courtship was short, and they moved in together several weeks after they met.

Alan was a teacher and Chris worked in a men's clothing store. Their early years together were marked by periodic blowups that Alan always had a hard time understanding because they seemed to come out of nowhere. It never occurred to Alan to look for a pattern to these altercations. He just decided that Chris was a volatile person who had to explode occasionally. Alan didn't like these occasions but he put up with them.

Around the fifth year of their relationship Alan became interested in a high school for gay and lesbian youth being started in their city. He began volunteering to teach there in his off hours. He loved the contact with the kids and felt that he was really giving back to his community in a way that was enjoyable as well as rewarding.

The more involved Alan became at the school the more trouble there was at home. Now the problems between him and Chris were not just periodic, they were almost continuous. One day Chris erased all of Alan's favorite videos. He was contrite. He said it had been an accident. Alan was furious. No way it could have been an accident.

Chris got into a fight with a neighbor and was so abusive the neighbor called the police. Alan had to go to the police station to bail Chris out. When Alan asked what had gotten into Chris the answer was vague, as though Chris didn't think it was a big deal that their neighbor was now their enemy. Alan was appalled and yelled at Chris, telling him to grow up.

The capper came when Alan brought home an armful of papers the students at the gay school had written on assignment from him. The next morning he couldn't find the papers though he was certain he'd left them on the dining room table. When asked, Chris said he hadn't seen them. Was Alan sure he'd brought them home?

Alan was distressed. The kids had worked hard on this assignment. He felt terrible. He couldn't imagine what had happened. Thinking he inadvertently might have put them in a drawer, he began going through both his desk and Chris's. In the bottom drawer of Chris's desk he found a small trash bag, the opening taped closed. Alan hesitated, but something told him he had to do this. He ripped the bag open. The students' papers were inside.

Alan was over the edge. When Chris came home from work Alan cornered him and began screaming at him. What right did he have to hide those papers? Was he crazy? Didn't he understand how important these kids were, how much he cared about working with them?

Chris just stared at Alan, looking hurt. He said he only wanted to look at the papers himself and he'd put them in the drawer for safekeeping. This was such an outrageous statement that Alan began to think that maybe Chris *was* crazy. He calmed down and insisted that Chris tell him exactly what was going on.

At first, Chris stuck to his story. He said he guessed he'd made a mistake by not telling Alan what he'd done with the papers. He was contrite. He apologized. But Alan was not buying it. He could no longer ignore Chris's behavior, and he was tired of the turmoil that they were so often in now. It almost seemed as if Chris *needed* him to be angry.

As they talked about what was happening, Chris finally said that he was feeling abandoned by Alan, who was spending so much time at the gay school. It felt to Chris as if Alan now cared more about those kids than he cared about him.

The light went on. Alan saw that the inexplicable bad behavior on Chris's part was his way of forcing Alan to pay attention to him. It had worked, but it had also caused Alan to become increasingly disaffected with the relationship. Because he *did* care about Chris, Alan decided to stay with him and try to understand why Chris had developed this crazy, self-defeating way of getting his needs met.

Realizing that Chris always felt as if he got what he deserved when Alan chastised him, Alan began to understand the dynamic involved. Chris got the *attention* he wanted and needed, and the anger and criticism were not only the price he had to pay but the mechanism for making it happen.

As they talked the discussion focused on how Chris had been brought up—how he had to work at getting his parents to acknowledge him, how he learned that being a bad kid got them to pay attention every time. With Alan's help Chris was eventually able to "reprogram" himself. He could get Alan's attention in a much less complicated way by just saying what he was feeling and what he needed. Chris's adult took charge of his bad kid.

THE SPOILED KID

Some parents are afraid of their children. Sounds strange, but it's true. These parents can't say no for fear that their children will not like them. Or they have the misguided notion that giving children everything they want will make them whole and happy human beings. Control is in the hands of the child. Discipline gives way to acquiescence. Conflict is avoided. It's the easy way out for these parents.

We've all known these people—adults with a spoiled kid inside. They expect to get their way because they always have. Compromise is a concept they do not easily grasp. They have a hard time in intimate relationships because the adjustment to another adult who does not defer to them is a difficult one.

Accustomed to being indulged, the person with the spoiled kid inside enters adulthood unprepared for real life. Why should anything be different from the way it's always been? The adult doesn't see a lover as an equal partner but as a provider.

The spoiled kid in the adult expects to be catered to, puts his or her needs first, and tends to exert control over much that happens in the relationship. There is little reason to consult about decisions affecting both people because spoiled kids usually end up having their way. Their parents did not have *no* in their vocabulary, and their partners are expected to be similarly agreeable to not denying them anything.

This arrangement does not work well unless one finds a partner who *wants* to be an indulgent parent and wants little more from a lover. Such partners do exist, and if there is no problem with the power imbalance, these two people can live happily ever after. But most adults want a relationship in which both the parent and the child in each partner have an equal chance to emerge and be experienced.

The spoiled kid may be powerful, like a parent, but he or she has little interest in being nurturing and fostering growth like a parent. The power involved here is that of the child who wins every disagreement by default. Parents give in to avoid conflict and bind their children to them.

All the spoiled kid knows is that he or she is at the center of the universe and can do no wrong. People who are in relationships with adults who were indulged and catered to as children have the challenge of not reinforcing the expectation of business as usual. The child within who is a spoiled kid *can* grow up with a partner who is willing to counter a misguided upbringing.

Phil and Joe

Phil was attracted to Joe because he was good-looking, charming, and talented, an irresistible combination for Phil. From the beginning, Phil was put off by Joe's demanding nature, but he was in love with him and that overshadowed everything else.

After they moved in together, Joe seemed to be less self-absorbed and more able to tune in to Phil's needs, but several years into the relationship Phil realized that the change was only an illusion fed by his own deep desire to see Joe not as the person he was but as the person he wanted him to be.

Joe's family was constantly in their lives, as though they needed their only child's presence to validate their own existence. Phil didn't dislike Joe's parents, but he found it odd that they seemed to require such an inordinate amount of Joe's attention and approval. Phil had a good relationship with his own parents, but he felt independent of them and they of him.

Whenever Joe wanted something of his parents, it was immediately produced. He wanted a car he couldn't afford to buy; Dad forked over the money. He was angry with Phil about something; Mom was there telling him that he was in the right. He wanted to go to Brazil on a trip that didn't interest Phil; Mom and Dad bought the tickets and went right along with him.

On the other hand, when Phil was offered a business trip to the Far East for which he would be gone a week, Joe had a fit, protesting that he had planned a trip to a resort that week and he didn't want to go alone. Of course, he hadn't informed Phil of the resort trip. He'd just made the plans, assuming that if he wanted to go Phil would want to go also.

It was about this time that Phil's feelings for Joe began to change. It was no longer possible to overlook the selfishness, Joe's disregard for anyone's needs but his own. Phil knew that he had to do something drastically different in the relationship if it was going to survive.

The theme of the discussion that Phil initiated with Joe was "That's enough. No more indulgence. I'm not going to cooperate with your selfishness anymore."

At first Joe didn't know what Phil was talking about. He didn't see himself as selfish. He just assumed that Phil adored him and wanted the best for him. How else should a lover be? Phil patiently explained to Joe, with many examples, the effect his self-absorbed behavior was having. He recounted story after story, highlighting Joe's habit of making plans without consulting him, not taking into account what Phil's interests or needs might be.

For a time Joe continued to deny that there was a problem, but Phil persisted. The break came the next time they planned a trip together. Joe was, in a sense, caught in the act. He went ahead, once again, and made arrangements organized around his needs without bothering to find out what Phil wanted to do.

Phil did not let Joe get away with it this time. There was no getting out of it. Joe had to acknowledge what he had done. In subsequent confrontations of this nature, Joe came to see that he did operate in a very self-absorbed way. Gritty as it was to do it, Phil stuck with his campaign to show Joe to himself.

When the discussion got around to Joe's parents and how they had catered to him all his life, Joe began to have a glimmer of insight into why he was the way he was. The best effect of this was that Joe was able to see that Phil, his adult lover, was distinct from Mom and Dad, his doting, overindulgent parents. They needed to earn his love with favors. Phil didn't. The partnership slowly became a more balanced affair—rooted in the present, shaped by the needs of both men, a growing relationship of peers.

THE MEAN KID

Gratuitous meanness can only be understood by culling out that child inside who had an upbringing in which parents dealt with their children by belittling and denigrating them. Perhaps these parents were following the only model they knew, or they were blaming their children for their own failures, or they were just so full of anger it spilled over onto their kids.

Mean parents produce mean children who cope with frustration by replicating what they have grown up with—attack, spoil your good time, tell you what's wrong with you, make you feel bad. When the mean kid takes over the censors stop working—anything can come out, the more hurtful the better.

The mean kid strikes, often blindly, in retaliation for being hurt again, anger stirred, reason gone, the focus only on delivering the retaliating blow. Sometimes it makes no sense. A lover, handy and vulnerable, makes a good target. Why? What triggers that child within, hurting still from the mockery of a parent, to lash out as if parent and lover were one?

Therein lies the mystery and its clues. The derision of a parent cuts deeply even if it is cloaked in some positive parental intent—"I just want to toughen my kids up to deal with life." What happens instead is that the parent gains a lock on the child's sense of self-esteem. The child/adult struggles against a phantom adversary, battling a self-negating image, trying to feel okay, and furious at the power still exerted by the belittling parent.

A close adult relationship, with many of the same elements of the parental bond, lures the mean kid out whenever there is what even *appears* to be derision by a partner. The mean kid isn't looking for love or approval at that moment, only retaliation. This child within is angry, and that anger is always there, close to the surface, easily tapped into, a defining emotion.

Mattie and Diondra

Mattie and Diondra got along well most of the time, but Mattie had never gotten used to the angry lashing out that Diondra did when she thought she was being put down. Mattie had to watch herself because even a benign joke could be interpreted as ridicule by Diondra and bring on a scathing verbal attack. Mattie didn't know what to do about Diondra in these situations. She endured the name-calling and the abusive language because she loved her partner, but she didn't like this mean streak in Diondra's personality.

Mattie didn't get to see much of Diondra's family because they lived in another part of the country. There were occasional visits, but they were always crowd scenes with the whole family gathered at once. Now Diondra's mother was coming to visit on her own, and Mattie was looking forward to getting to know her better. She couldn't have guessed how much better that was going to be.

On the first day of the visit they took Diondra's mother shopping at the mall. In a clothing store, Diondra's mother suggested that her daughter should think about buying some new clothes because she dressed strangely and looked like a Gypsy. Diondra said nothing. When they later passed a beauty shop, the mother suggested that Diondra try going in there sometime because the way she wore her hair made her look like someone on a psychiatric ward. Again Diondra said nothing.

As Mattie led them into a bookstore, Diondra's mother laughed and said, "Does this mean my child has learned to read at last? She was such a bad student I thought we had a retard on our hands." Mattie just stared at the silent Diondra.

Mattie was beginning to feel quite tense about these cruel remarks, but Diondra said nothing and showed no emotion. That night, when the two were alone, Mattie told Diondra that she was uncomfortable with her lover's mother's criticisms. Diondra blew up.

"You're uncomfortable! All you ever think about is yourself! You are a selfish, egotistical bitch! You don't care about my feelings at all!"

And Mattie suddenly understood that Diondra was

talking to her mother, spewing out the anger she had been unable to show in her mother's presence. Mattie's mind flashed back to many situations in which Diondra had verbally attacked her when she was not aware of having done anything to deserve it. Diondra was like a little kid at these times, but with the power of an adult to wound with words.

For the rest of their visit Mattie continued to observe how Diondra's mother belittled and ridiculed her daughter and how Diondra seethed quietly inside without fighting back. One thing was soon different, however. Mattie decided to no longer allow Diondra to express her anger at her mother by being mean to her.

Perhaps it was Diondra's having her mother right there or perhaps it was Mattie's unusually firm tone, but Diondra seemed to hear Mattie and make the connection between her mother's behavior and her own. Even so, it took a long period of coming back to this point before Diondra's *behavior* changed significantly. She was able to get her reactions in perspective, seeing that so often they were out of proportion to what was happening.

The tension in the relationship eased without the potential of one of Diondra's blow-ups being imminent. By mutual agreement, the two women decided that the less they saw of Diondra's mother the better off everyone would be.

THE BALANCING ACT

It is the rare person who does not still have that child within who at times demands attention, complicates simple transactions, and confuses anybody operating on the notion that we are all rational human beings. These

kids are the products of the unfinished business of childhood. Whatever was missing or went wrong forms something irrational in the adult who may otherwise be quite
sane, stable, and mature.

The kids who cause trouble are those who have never
been fully integrated into the adult. Of course, they are
not always so clearly delineated as I have shown here,
and they are not necessarily mutually exclusive. You may
have several of these kids competing for your attention.

So how do you balance child versus adult? How do
you learn to integrate that part of yourself that has
stayed separate and operates subversively, pleading always for more love and reassurance, unable to share,
fearful of life, or angry and vindictive? How do you take
the power away from the child and put it back in the
hands of the adult?

First comes awareness, the willingness and ability to
be introspective enough to consider if any of this might
be true of you. Awareness is the essential prelude to behavior change; it clears the way for seeing where the
child ends and the adult begins. Subtle as these internal
dramas usually are, they have an undeniable force once
brought into play.

For instance, you are trying to get something you
want from your lover, who is being stubborn and uncom-
promising. You are frustrated. You try harder. It does no
good. This is familiar territory to the needy kid within
you. You retreat into your hurt feelings, preoccupied
with deprivation and the fear that you will never have
what you need. You withdraw and pout for a while and
then begin seeking reassurance that you are at least still
loved.

What is the alternative to this unrewarding scenario?
You might find out why your lover is being so unforth-

coming. You might ask: "What is going on?" You can turn up the volume on your request, insist on a response rather than disappearing into your child. You can call up your adult to remain engaged until you get what you want.

This is the balancing act, the process by which you can slowly integrate the aggrieved child into the functioning adult. Observe yourself in action. Are you behaving in a way that is getting you nowhere? Have you asked yourself why you keep doing things that cause people close to you to become impatient, irritated, or hurt?

If your spoiled kid is in charge, do you really want the resentment that comes with being unwilling to compromise? Is your scared kid dictating self-protective action instead of allowing you to take risks and have new experiences? How about a bad kid getting you into trouble you don't want to be in, or a mean kid blindly attacking someone you really want to love you?

These may be disturbing ideas, too overdrawn to consider that they might be relevant for you. I understand that. I don't want to believe that the fears with which I struggle in my life are the products of a scared kid inside of me whom I have to balance with my rational adult. I'd rather not think that I was taught as a child to be so afraid of life that I grew up to be a worrier, self-protective and overly vigilant.

I'd rather not think of myself in this flawed way, but I cannot deny that in relationships I have acted out of a motivation I sometimes didn't understand. I have run away from certain aspects of life because it never occurred to me to do it any other way.

Now, when I find myself poised for flight, or giving in to fear, I know better. I have a dialogue going with the scared kid, who has lost much of her influence because

I acknowledge her presence and her power. She can't sneak up on me so easily anymore. I don't deny her and she doesn't control me. She may fear abandonment but I am secure in the elements of my life. The balancing act is working.

CHAPTER 5

Talking It Over—Constructive Complaining, Differences and Disputes, Healing the Wounds

"Conversation is the sex act of the soul, and as such it is supremely conducive to the cultivation of intimacy."

So writes Thomas Moore in his book *Soul Mates: Honoring the Mysteries of Love and Relationship*. The need to communicate is as strong in most people as the needs to be safe, productive, and valued. Prominent psychologists Carl Rogers and Sidney Jourard have written at length about the force behind the impulse to disclose ourselves to others. This is a major reason why psychotherapy works, why we sometimes tell our innermost feelings to strangers on airplanes, and why hordes of irregular folk are on television daily pouring out their tales of familial disorder.

Of course, we might say that the patient in psychotherapy is just trying to grow, the airplane confessant is lonely, and those unenviable creatures on the talk shows are exhibitionists. That's probably true, but all of these people are motivated to talk about themselves because the desire to become known is so basic to human functioning. Create the opportunity, and people will talk. There doesn't even have to be a person on the other end, as is demonstrated by the following.

Years ago, when I was working with Carl Rogers, we set up a room at a conference in which there was nothing but a single chair and a table with a voice-activated tape recorder on it. Participants were invited to come into the room and talk about themselves. No reason for doing this was given, no purpose outlined, no information offered about what would be done with the tapes.

The room was in use almost twenty-four hours a day. People talked about their lives, their fears, their dreams, and their frustrations. They told stories and painted word pictures of the people they loved and hated. I suppose the assumption was that someone would eventually listen to the tapes, but the extraordinary thing was that, with no immediate response, no feedback, these people sitting in an empty room kept right on talking. The satisfaction seemed to be in the act of disclosing, and the motivation appeared to be simply the opportunity to do so.

There are situations in all of our lives in which we talk, having no great expectation that we will be responded to. For example, small talk at parties is designed primarily to give people a nondemanding way of making contact. The content is not as important as the form, and since there is always the possibility of being interrupted, superficiality is the appropriate level to aim for.

With friends and relatives (the good kind) we do expect to be responded to, because our connections with them are a crucial link to reality. We stay in touch mainly by talking about one another's lives. We try to avoid controversy and confrontation. The objective is to preserve these relationships in good order because they are our bulwark against isolation and loneliness.

No matter whom we are talking to, many of us spend time telling our stories.

"Here's who I am."
"Here's who I was."
"Here's what has happened to me."

Reminiscences, reflections on the past, and nostalgia for a lost era are common ways to tie our current existence to our history, to identify who we are to ourselves and to others. We want to tell our tales so that others can know us as we have been, and we want to be heard and responded to as we offer our stories to inform, amuse, bring glory to ourselves, or enlist compassion.

The trouble is . . . we are sometimes telling our stories to people who have heard them before. How could I have forgotten that I told my lover the story about that particular escapade half a dozen times over the last twenty-two years? And what is she supposed to do when I launch into it?

Should she say, "Stop, I've heard that story enough!"

Or, more gently, "Oh, yes, you did tell me about that before."

My own lover says she listens out of politeness, but I don't want her to do that. Since she has heard the story before, her response can hardly be as enthusiastic as it was for the first (or second or third) telling. Most likely her response will be polite but flat. I then take that to mean that she was not informed or amused by my story. On a really bad hair day I would interpret her flat reply as evidence that she's just not interested in *anything* I tell her.

What would be much better than politeness would be honesty. If I have a burning need to tell my story anyway, at least I will have the opportunity to reshape and reinterpret it for a different emphasis and a new message. And I can be reminded that it would be a good idea to preface my next story with "Have I ever told you . . . ?"

THE SILENT PARTNER

"I feel as if I'm invisible when I get no response."
"I might as well be talking to the wall!"
"You are doing this to drive me crazy!"

The silent partner is the one who mentally processes what is being said but tends not to, or is slow to, put words to the thoughts. One person tells a story, makes a comment, or talks about feelings, and the other sits quietly saying nothing. I have seen reactions from the partner who is not being responded to that range from annoyance to rage.

Why do people sometimes give their lovers the silent treatment? What is going on here? Often what is happening with silent partners is that they are mulling over the right response—stuck in their head, lost in a maze of thoughts. Whatever ideas or comments they have about what has been said they tell to themselves. When questioned, they say things like "Well, I *was* listening. I was just thinking about what you said."

The unresponded-to partner may come to feel lonely and isolated if this happens often enough. The need to "talk this over" becomes acute. The silent partner must learn to accept that there are no right answers, that no one is sitting in judgment of the discussion, that most people need something more than the echo of their own voice to feel okay. It is time for what I call "constructive complaining."

CONSTRUCTIVE COMPLAINING

"To express grief, pain or discontent" is how the dictionary defines *complain*. What would make such a lament *constructive* would be if you didn't stop with the complaint but added what you would like to change, what you need to happen to feel okay. Constructive complaining is not just ordinary kvetching with no objective. It is a focused attempt to bring to your partner's attention something that you are bothered by and need to have changed.

Let's go back to the example of the silent partner. What do you do when you have a lover who doesn't say anything to acknowledge that you have just spoken, whether it is the most mundane comment or something of great importance to you?

Rebecca Cutter, in her thought-provoking book *When Opposites Attract: Right Brain/Left Brain Relationships and How to Make Them Work*, offers a remedy called "bridging."

Bridging is accomplished by the utterance of phrases that in essence promote progress, ease the flow, and demonstrate connection at the same time. . . . Common bridging terms are: "Uh-huh," "Um-hmm," "Yes," "Right," "Go on," "Then?" "Tell me more," and "Really?" The beauty of bridging phrases is that they offer the listening partner a mechanism with which to encourage his partner to continue without having to construct a lengthy response or even agree with what is being said. By periodically uttering

one of these, the listening partner is saying, "I am following you. You have my full attention. Your words are being
received."

So what may begin as a complaint is followed up by
a discussion of the behavior in question (or lack of behavior) and the changes being asked for. Sometimes it is
necessary to go back over the territory a number of
times, especially if you are dealing with someone's lifelong habit.

It also can be helpful to "model" the behavior you
want to see. For instance, if your partner is unresponsive
you can be sure to *always* respond when he or she says
anything to you.

Another version of the silent-partner problem is the
person who, upon hearing your story, says nothing, asks
nothing, but uses what you have said as a cue to tell a
story of his or her own. You are left stranded—no response, no attempt to find out more from you. What you
had to say was simply a launching pad for the other person to take their turn. What are you left with?

"My story wasn't interesting enough to comment on?"
"You don't care enough about what is happening to me to
  even acknowledge that I have told you something?"

This, too, can be a lonely and isolating experience
when you are trying to share your feelings or perhaps
just to get some feedback on an encounter you've had.
You finish your last sentence, and your partner, without
taking a breath, launches into his or her "turn." This is
a time for constructive complaining: "But wait. I need to
hear what you think about what I just said."

The importance of constructive complaining turns
on the principle of authenticity in relationships. As

daunting as expressing discontent may be, it is infinitely better than retreating into silence, thus compromising your own authentic need for change.

For some people retreat from conflict is learned early and reinforced frequently in the family: "I wasn't raised that way. No one in my family complained about anything. I was taught to grin and bear it, forgive and forget, turn the other cheek."

If a grin-and-bear-it family culture is keeping you from dealing with the dissatisfaction in your relationship, it is time to think about who you are now versus who you were back then. The code of silence about domestic dramas that some families impose on their children can become a lifelong strategy to minimize or deny anything that might create or reveal tension on the home front.

Helen and Susan

Helen came from a family in which it was considered rude and inappropriate to criticize or complain about anything that went on among family members. Since Helen's father was an alcoholic who periodically created chaos in the household, there was plenty to complain about. But no one did. There was no talk inside or outside the family about the father's behavior or the mother's despair during the drinking bouts that caused everyone to turn inward, pretending that nothing unusual was happening.

Helen's partner, Susan, came from a family that was comfortable dealing with their conflicts and expressing dissatisfaction with the behavior of other family members. When Helen and Susan had a problem, Helen would go about the house in silence, avoiding Susan, looking as if she were preoccupied with something too important to interrupt.

Susan had become accustomed to Helen's avoidance behavior, but lately she was feeling more frustrated than usual. In their years together there had been very little conflict to deal with, but recently Susan had begun to travel more for her job and was away from home a lot. Though Helen said nothing, it was obvious that she was unhappy about being alone so much. She had a long face and spoke little when Susan was at home.

Susan felt herself growing tenser about what was happening. Finally, she could stand it no longer. She decided to break the code. She confronted Helen, asking what her feelings were about the frequent absences. Helen smiled and said quietly that there wasn't a problem. Susan found herself becoming angry. When she was at home she wanted companionship and warmth, and what she was getting from Helen was a cold shoulder.

Unable to break through, Susan suggested they go to a counselor. Helen was horrified. Talk to a stranger about their personal life? She couldn't imagine doing that. Susan did what she didn't usually do: She allowed her anger to come through in full force. She told Helen how she felt about being given the silent treatment. She said that her feelings for Helen were so affected by this that she didn't want to be near her because it had become too painful. That got Helen's attention, and she agreed to go for counseling.

As Helen was able to open up in therapy and talk about her early training—the code of silence in the family, the denial of a troubling reality—she began to make the connections to her mode of dealing with problems in her relationship with Susan. They went over this territory again and again until Helen could see how her avoidance of anything negative with Susan was sabotaging her ability to relate freely to her partner.

With Susan's help—not allowing Helen to get away with withdrawal behavior—Helen was able to move on from her early models and chance the kind of confrontation she had learned to avoid at all costs. The idea of her lover's needing to avoid her was enough to motivate her to do the hard work of changing a lifelong way of coping with conflict.

No adult needs to remain a prisoner of his or her family history. If you cannot sort out then from now on your own, think about getting some professional help to do that. It will be worth it if it can free you from the fear of expressing feelings that may be an obstacle to a deeper bond with the person you love.

DIFFERENCES AND DISPUTES

Because there are so many built-in differences between men and women, there is a complementariness that assumes and accepts difference. In same-sex partnerships, differences seem to stand out, to perplex, to irritate more because they defy the expectation of sameness. Many disputes of gay and lesbian couples have their origins in what may seem like intolerable differences between the partners. What it all comes down to is: *"Why can't you be like me?"*

This is the lament that so often distills out of the dissatisfactions of a relationship. Why-can't-you-be-like-me plays out in large concerns—such as out in the world, relating to friends and family, planning for the future—and in smaller issues—such as wishing your partner could get as excited as you do about this movie, that book, or the new person you just met.

For some couples this conflict about differences is at the level of annoyance; for others it is a major obstacle to maintaining a satisfying and loving life together. The partner who longs for *sameness* may feel put off when the other person has a different reaction to something they have experienced together, but disagreement does not equal rejection, and differences in taste, style, and interests do not mean that a couple is incompatible.

What might be looked into when these issues arise is the deeper meaning of seeming not to be validated: "If you don't like what I like, don't want what I want, don't think as I do, I feel invalidated. I will then most likely fault you for your stubbornness or lack of taste, but what I really should be looking at is my own need to have my worth affirmed by having a partner who is willing to be almost *another me.*"

We all have a need to be validated, but some of us have more of a need because we did not get our value mirrored back to us sufficiently when we were forming our images of who we are. When this has been true, there is a tendency to worry our adult transactions for evidence that we are desirable, respected, and loved.

Having a partner who can validate us becomes particularly crucial, but when validation is mixed up with an intolerance of differences, there is trouble in the making. There must be freedom in intimate relationships to differ, to be different, and to express differences without being accused of invalidating one's partner: "Validate me with your love and your presence, not by agreeing with everything I say and think and do."

For purposes of making the point I have focused on a somewhat extreme aspect of this dilemma. Of course, we all want to be with someone who has a similar worldview and interests in common, but when differences do emerge the remedy is the same whether it's about a simple difference of opinion or the unfinished business of childhood. The remedy, the mantra, the solution of choice: talk it over.

NEGOTIATING FOR CHANGE

Sometimes talking it over isn't quite enough. A more sophisticated level of discussion is called for involving the art of negotiation. Most people would probably say that they already know how to negotiate for what they want. No doubt true, but in the tangled web of emotions that any intimate relationship can be, negotiation may go awry. Understanding why this happens can help to get back on track and stay there until the transaction is completed.

The following ideas are based on the work of the Harvard [University] Negotiation Project, as described in *Getting Together: Building Relationships As We Negotiate* by Roger Fisher and Scott Brown.

First, you must begin with the premise that *change is possible.* If you do not believe this, there is no point in negotiating. If you have convinced yourself that your partner will never change and you use that notion to avoid dealing directly with your dissatisfactions in the relationship, you are cheating your partner and yourself.

Second, you must open to the possibility that there could be *something new* for you to learn. We all like to think of ourselves as open-minded, but in the crunch we often tend to cling to our points of view as if they were the last life rafts in a stormy sea. I personally have been startled when my partner tells me something in the heat of conflict that is truly new to me, that I would not have imagined on my own. It is not always easy (but it is crucial to resolving conflict and strengthening your relationship) to keep a part of your brain open to hear what you may not have known before.

When negotiation doesn't get off the ground or breaks down in midstream, it is usually for one or more of the following reasons:

1. Assuming there is no need to talk. One partner may decide that she or he already knows what the other person will say and what the decision *should* be, and therefore concludes that in the final analysis the other person will renege on making a decision anyway.

What is ignored in this assumption is the possibility that the second partner may feel devalued by being left out, have different and better information to contribute, and end up feeling coerced into a decision rather than consulted about it. Assuming that there is no need to engage a partner in negotiation because you can just as easily make the decision yourself is hazardous to the good standing of any intimate relationship.

Jon and Michael

Jon wants Michael to help him entertain some out-of-town people important to his work. He knows Michael loves to cook and have people over, and he knows they have a free night on Saturday, so he goes ahead and invites a small group for dinner. After they have all accepted, he tells Michael, who hits the ceiling. Michael says that he resents being part of an evening in his own home that he had no part in initiating.

Michael: *"Why didn't you talk to me about it first?"*
Jon: *"What is there to talk about? You like to cook. We're free that night. What's the problem?"*

Michael: "The problem is that I wasn't consulted."

Jon: "What's to consult? I thought you would agree, but if not . . . well, I had no choice, the decision had to be made right away and I was the one to make it."

Michael: "Did it ever occur to you that I might not feel like cooking for a whole group of people when I will be playing in a tennis tournament that afternoon? You can't assume there is nothing to talk about and just make plans. I resent your taking me for granted that way. You'll have to make other plans."

Michael felt trivialized by his partner and angered at the assumption that there was no need to consult him. He was in anything but a negotiating mood, wanting only to let Jon know how inconsiderate he was being.

2. Communicating in one direction only. Some people are compelled to talk. Once they get started they go on and on, neglecting to give the other person a chance to respond. They throw up a wall of words. A partner must then either work hard to penetrate the wall or shut down and stop listening. In either case the exchange of information that is essential for change to occur is stalled. People who talk *at* others often do so to protect themselves. It is a way to control what is happening, to avoid having to deal with someone else's needs or conflicting opinions.

Alice and Nancy

Alice was an inveterate talker. She always had something to say. When Nancy tried to talk to Alice about something she wanted to negotiate, she was hardly able to get a sentence out before Alice interrupted her. Nancy would fall silent for a while. Then she would take a deep breath and try again, soon to be interrupted and inundated by another torrent of words from Alice.

Sometimes Nancy would begin screaming at Alice, who was always startled by this.

> Alice: *"Why are you screaming at me?"*
> Nancy: *"Because you don't stop talking long enough for me to say what I have to say."*
> Alice: *"Nonsense. You can say whatever you want, but let me tell you first that . . ."*

Often Nancy would just give up and let Alice talk, her mind all but shut down, trying to listen but too full of annoyance to absorb the meaning of what Alice was saying. She understood that Alice was a talker, but the wall of words was building a barrier between them. Nancy felt closed out and frustrated. Worn down by Alice's domination of the discussion, Nancy usually had neither the energy not the motivation to try to negotiate in these situations.

It is incumbent on the partner being talked at to interrupt in order to become a participant in the discussion. This person's focus should be on the feelings elicited by listening to a barrage of thoughts, feelings, and opinions and not being given equal time to respond. Why put the burden on the "victim"? If the person doing the talking had a better perspective on this behavior, he or she probably wouldn't be so busy throwing up the wall of words in the first place.

3. Sending mixed messages. When a partner is inconsistent in his or her statements, it is difficult to maintain trust in that person. Contradictory messages raise questions about what is going on. Inconsistency may occur because the person has conflicting agendas, is concerned about short-term versus long-term needs, or wants to be truthful but is worried about hurting the other person's feelings.

Being honest and direct about conflicting interests or feelings is preferable to sending mixed messages that confuse and cause distrust.

Saying "I want to talk to you about what happened, but I don't want to hurt your feelings" is better than skirting the issue or pretending there is really nothing to talk about when it is obvious to everyone that there is.

We are all in the sway of competing needs and agendas at one time or another. Being in touch with this kind of conflict within ourselves can do a lot to dispel the confusion that arises when our messages conflict with one another.

For instance, you may feel perfectly willing to negotiate with a partner, but let's say you are also in a power struggle with this person. One message is that you are open to suggestions; the other is that you are going to be in control of what happens. Unless you are tuned in to these competing agendas from within yourself, you may create a climate of confusion that makes negotiation impossible.

4. Attacking the individual versus attacking the problem. It is tempting to attack the person you are in discussion with rather than the problem you are in discussion about. Perhaps you are angry about being disagreed with, or having your competence questioned, or having to deal with this issue at all.

You zero in on your "opponent" in an effort to discredit or disarm the person. What happens to the problem to be solved? It may *feel* good to get in your blows, but negotiation comes to a halt in the process.

Newt and Marlon

Newt wants to take a vacation in August. Marlon wants to go later in the year. Marlon says to Newt, "Are you crazy? You want to go to a national park when school is out and all those kids are running around? You have no sense. Sometimes I wonder how you get through the day. I've never known anyone so unrealistic."

Newt responds in kind, and soon the discussion has spiraled out of control, the partners vying to top each other's insults. Vacation plans are all but forgotten.

A better transaction would be the following:

"How about this instead?" Marlon would say to Newt. "Let's think about going in October, when the little dears are back in school."

And Newt says, "You're right about the kids, but I feel frustrated. I'd really like to go to a national park while it's still warm. Maybe we could go right after school starts."

And soon plans are under way for a mutually agreed upon vacation.

5. *Winning a contest versus solving a problem.* Negotiation should be treated as joint problem-solving, not as a contest that one partner wins and the other loses. Are these two people on the same side or on opposing sides? How easy it is to slip into the mind-set that the goal is to *win* the argument.

What argument? I thought we were solving a problem here! Partners who see disagreements as having a winner and a loser need to be reminded that collaboration rather than competition is what makes intimate partnerships work. One of the gifts of relationship is the experience of having someone on your side. There may be two sides to the problem, but there is only one side to be on—each other's.

6. *Either/or versus multiple options.* The more choices are limited in a negotiation, the more adversarial the encounter is likely to become and the less likely it is that a mutually satisfying outcome will be achieved.

If I tell you it has to be this way or that way and that's it, you are probably going to feel coerced and take a similarly either/or position. Now we are into a tug-of-war rather than a negotiation.

The more productive approach is for both of us to generate options and variations on those options. This moves the discussion away from a struggle to win and implies that we are mutually committed to finding the best solution for both of us.

Del and Marsha

Del and Marsha were struggling with a decision about allowing Del's former lover to be a houseguest. Marsha had never met Francine and was not keen on having her in their home. Del thought this was petty, since her relationship with Francine had been over for years. Marsha admitted that her attitude might be irrational; nevertheless, she was not comfortable with having Del's ex-lover around. Del was adamant about wanting to be hospitable to Francine. They began to negotiate.

Del said, "Look, you have two choices. Either she stays here or she stays in a hotel and I spend much of the time that she's in town away from home going places with her."

Marsha answered, "Oh, great, those are my choices? Thanks a lot. Well, I reject both choices. You can't just force me to accept what you want. I have something to say, and I say no Francine in our lives, period."

Del declared that the conversation was over. She would just have to decide on her own what she was going to do.

A more successful negotiation would have been the following:

> *Del: "I know you have some feelings about Francine being here, but she is really a nice person and I want you to enjoy her. She is no threat to us. She can certainly stay in a hotel, but if she stays here we can both be with her and I won't have to spend time away from you, which I don't want to do."*
>
> *Marsha: "I'll agree to her staying here if it's just for a few days, not the whole week she wants."*
>
> *Del: "I'll ask her to do that. Will you help me plan what to do while she's here?"*
>
> *Marsha: "I'll help if you'll not try to argue me out of my feelings and don't try to push me at her."*
>
> *Del: "I promise I won't do that. You can be with her as much or as little as you want."*
>
> *Marsha: "Fair enough. I'm willing to try this."*

These are some of the barriers to successful negotiation that partners encounter in relationships. For the dos as well as the don'ts of effective negotiation, see my earlier book, *Permanent Partners: Building Gay and Lesbian Relationships That Last.*

HEALING THE WOUNDS

It is hard to imagine any gay or lesbian person living in our homophobic society who has not been wounded by the hostility that prevails against us. Sometimes the wounding comes from family, sometimes from strangers or coworkers or those who simply inhabit a nearby space to ours.

It may be words that are hurtful or a particularly negative portrayal in the media or the laughter of unknowing children. Too often the injury is physical, as if pounding on the body of a gay person might eradicate the fear of sexual confusion in the perpetrator.

Subtle, ambiguous, or explicitly hate-induced, the wounds that gay and lesbian people must endure are the price we pay for following our hearts. Where is our refuge? Certainly in our partnerships? Not always. For a relationship to work and endure, a certain amount of vulnerability on the part of both partners is essential. Unless there is this openness to the other person the relationship will have no soul. But it is this very openness, this vulnerability, that creates the potential for lovers to wound *one another.*

Indeed, our community, our friendships, and our lovers are the bulwarks we need to thrive in a nonaccepting society. Our community is growing and growing up but is inconsistent in the protections it offers us. Our friends cannot always be there for us even though they mean to. That leaves our lovers to depend on for solace and comfort.

It is actually almost inevitable that at some time we will be wounded by the person closest to us—hurt, inadvertently perhaps, by his or her insensitivity, negligence, or anger. The wound may tap into the reservoir of discomfort we all have about ourselves, and then something more than an apology is called for—a healing experience is needed. That experience must involve feelings communicated, an exchange of information, and evidence that both have been heard.

Active Listening

The ability to listen actively is an essential ingredient of communication, even if what you are hearing is some guilt-producing condemnation of yourself and the pain and anger your partner has suffered as a consequence. Listening actively means you are totally present—your mind is not wandering off the subject, you are not busy composing your next comments, you are not comforting yourself by thinking about what a damn fool your partner is. You are really listening.

In order to demonstrate to your partner that you are hearing what is being said you could ask questions to invite more information, or feed back the feelings that are being expressed.

> "You're really pissed off at me."
> "What was there about what I said that hurt you so much?"

An important aspect of listening actively is that you are not interrupting with comments that amount to "I don't want to hear any more about this."

For instance, arguing points defensively before the other person has a chance to get her or his whole story out cuts off the partner's opportunity to say what she or he needs to say. Prematurely reassuring that "it will never happen again" is often meant to stem the flow of the other's comments more than anything else.

Problem solving while the other person is talking about feelings is also abortive, unless you have been *invited* to give advice. Few remarks will chill a presentation of emotional material quicker than the other person's jumping in with

"Why don't you . . ."
"Have you thought of . . ."

For many people, listening to another in an emotionally loaded situation is difficult because they are so busy listening to their own inner messages.

"I don't need this."
"Why does she have to bring this up now?"
"I'm tired of his complaining."

Let's say you are faced with competing needs such as these:

"I want to listen to what my lover has to say."
"I want to get as far away from this as I can."

If the discussion is about something you have done that has wounded your partner, the healing choice is to stay, to be present, to listen.

In the red-hot moments of an argument, listening may be hard to do. But there are those moments just after the red-hots cool down, when you are no longer in a defensive mode and can ask for a reiteration of the issues. Now you can listen without arguing, defending, or setting the record straight. You can *hear* the feelings, absorb the information, and give your partner evidence that the communication has been received. The message is a healing one.

"Your feelings are important to me because I love you."

LETTING GO OF THE OLD IRRITANTS

The tenacity with which some couples hold on to ancient wounds often amazes me. Where healing such wounds would seem the most desirable course of action, these partners cling instead to the root cause of their anger. Learning to let go of these old irritants can be one of the most healing experiences a couple can have.

Roy and Eric

A male couple who had been together for sixteen years came to see me. I asked Roy and Eric what had brought them to me, and Roy answered that it was about "George." It seemed that Eric had met George on a business trip, and they had begun a romance that quickly grew hot and heavy.

At first Eric didn't tell Roy what was happening, but inevitably Roy became curious about Eric's frequent trips to the same city and Eric finally revealed the truth. He said he was involved, but he planned to end the affair. Roy was hurt and insisted that this ending happen sooner rather than later. Eric complied, though somewhat reluctantly, and the relationship with Roy gradually resumed the primacy it had before, though with an added degree of tension.

I asked why the affair was still a problem in their relationship since it was over. Roy said that he had not been satisfied with Eric's explanation of what got him involved with George, and he was still angry at Eric for the time he had spent away from their relationship. The surprise came when I asked when this affair with George had taken place. The answer was ten years before!

These two had been battling over the George episode for ten years, and it had all the energy of something that had happened yesterday. What purpose was served by this episode's being preserved to go back to over and over? As we worked, it became apparent that

Roy had current dissatisfactions with Eric that he had been unable to articulate for fear that Eric would become angry and seek another affair. It was just easier to keep going back to George.

Roy and Eric needed to see how they were using the past to avoid dealing with the present. For Roy it was difficult to be upfront about his dissatisfactions. He felt anxious and looked away from Eric when he finally began to talk about his feelings.

Roy had done such a good job of covering up that Eric was shocked when he heard Roy say that he was feeling abandoned because Eric didn't seem to want to spend time with him anymore. Eric's perception was very different. He thought that Roy was avoiding *him*. The issue of how interested each was currently in the other's companionship got lost as the retreaded tale of Eric's indiscretion with George seemed always to take over the discussion.

In *Permanent Partners* I wrote at length about "the theater of the relationship"—when dealing with real issues is avoided by focusing on a familiar conflict that has never been resolved but can be depended upon to take the time and energy that should be invested in a contemporary problem. As in a theatrical production, the dialogue is always the same, the path to the outcome never varied.

Some people hang on to a partner's past transgressions to justify hurt and angry feelings that appropriately belong to something in the present that is too difficult to talk about. Exploring what that something might be, and dealing with it, is a major way to clear a relationship of old irritants.

You might be thinking now, "But I really *am* still mad about what happened five years ago!" If that is the case,

I suggest you think about what fears might be associated with that anger that would have application in the present. Let's say your lover had an affair five years ago but quickly terminated it, apologized, and has been faithful and devoted ever since. But you still keep going back in your mind to what happened *then*.

"I can't let go of it," I hear people say.

What is often at stake is not the old affair but the concern that there will be a new one. *That* is what should be talked about. You can't rewrite history, but you can have an influence on what happens to you in the future. Get the reassurance you need, come back for more if you must, but don't get caught on a merry-go-round that turns to the tune of ancient discord. The present deserves all the attention it can get.

Anita and Becky

These two women were a couple admired by all their friends because they had been together fifteen years and appeared to have a trouble-free relationship. They were in business together, they traveled, had a beautiful home, entertained, and always seemed happy to be in each other's presence. They were—except for one month out of the year, when theirs became the relationship from hell.

Two years earlier, on the Fourth of July, Anita and Becky had attended a party at a friend's house. The liquor flowed and everyone was in high spirits. At one point Becky was dancing with a woman whose name she didn't even know. They had just found each other on the dance floor and begun dancing, and silently continued dancing for a long time.

Becky felt something different happening to her, an

excitement that she hadn't felt in a long time. It didn't even matter that she didn't know who this woman was. The only thing that mattered was that they were supposed to be dancing together, or so it seemed. The music stopped and started again. The two women drew closer and continued to dance.

Suddenly Becky realized that almost an hour had passed. She felt self-conscious, wondering where Anita was, embarrassed that she and the nameless woman had become so involved. She excused herself and went in search of Anita.

Becky found Anita quite engaged with other people, apparently unaware of Becky's encounter on the dance floor. Reassured, Becky wandered off, not really searching for her dance partner, but delighted when she did run into her. The two women talked and made plans to have lunch together. That was the beginning of an affair that lasted all of six weeks, Becky calling it off when her guilt became more affecting than her attraction to the woman.

It seemed that Becky had gotten away with her dalliance, but that was not to be—thanks to one of those "friends," who discovered the affair and considered it her righteous duty to inform Anita that her lover was involved with another woman.

There was a painful confrontation, and Becky told Anita the whole truth, including the fact that the affair had ended. That didn't help, however. Anita was hurt and angry and thought seriously about leaving the relationship. Becky talked her out of throwing away a wonderful life for something that was over and wouldn't happen again.

Eventually, life returned to normal for the two women, but an odd thing happened when the next July rolled around—Anita became tense and angry and shut

Becky out of their bedroom. It didn't seem to make any sense, but Anita was reliving the pain she had felt the previous year when she thought she was losing her lover. It was as if the trauma was reawakened by the anniversary of the triggering event. The entire month was misery for both women.

Again, life eventually returned to normal, but the following July the drama repeated itself. Becky insisted they get help, and they came to see me. Both women agreed it was crazy for Anita to go through the anguish she did about something that was over and done with. Anita said she couldn't help herself. She found that she was overwhelmed with anxiety when she thought about losing her partner.

Becky just looked incredulous when Anita said this. She insisted that she had no intention of ever leaving Anita, who came back with, "But you did leave me. How do I know you won't do it again?"

This refrain continued for many sessions until Anita was able to see in herself the source of her anxiety—the idea that she could be abandoned and alone. Becky's constant reassurances did not touch the real fears Anita had about her own attractiveness and competence as a partner.

Once this truth was uncovered, Becky and Anita could deal with the fears, and Anita was able to integrate Becky's love for her into her own picture of herself. Finally, Anita could let go of the old wound. I was seeing them when the next Fourth of July came. The anniversary trigger had lost its power. The focus was on the present, on the good life they had and would continue to share.

There is always the potential in our relationships to wound and be wounded. Usually we don't mean to be hurtful, but many of us are more fragile than we care to admit. "Handle with care," the package should read. When the message is unreadable, or even known but ignored, the only remedy, the healing act, is to talk about it. Doing this, no matter how difficult it seems, is an exercise of faith in your own and your partner's ability to move on, to build trust, to create a deeper and more fulfilling alliance.

CHAPTER 6

Sex in the Long Term—
Its Delights and Dilemmas

Sex in the long term *is* different from the flashy erotic encounters that we remember from our own early adventures—and sometimes dream of returning to when our relationship hits the sexual doldrums. Sex in the long term is an expression of the deeper love that grows with time and the intimate knowledge of another's being. It is a collaborative journey to a familiar place of desire and pleasuring where nothing has to be proved, no prizes are at stake, and the emotional primacy of each to the other is assured.

But while time is usually the deepening agent in a couple's love, it can also at times be a spoiler that shuts down desire and challenges ingenuity to find ways to keep sex alive. Once lust leaves the mind it is difficult to resurrect. But lust should be only the opening act, the warm-up to a kind of companionate love that creates its own erotic triggers. The trouble is, these triggers do not always go on firing on their own.

SIX ENEMIES OF SEXUAL DESIRE
IN LONG-TERM RELATIONSHIPS

THE THRILL IS GONE

For people who have spent too much time in the arena of single sex, with its emphasis on the hunt, sex with a willing and available partner can sometimes lose its appeal after the initial passion is over. Sex may become too easy, lacking the excitement of the conquest. If an important element of one's sex life had been the incentive to "score," relationship sex could be too routine and predictable.

THE INCEST TABOO

In her book *Peer Marriages: How Love Between Equals Really Works*, sociologist Pepper Schwartz writes:

For a few, there is the creation of something very much like an incest taboo. Sex may suffer if the "best friend" identity of a spouse overwhelms the identity of lover. . . . The challenge for peer couples is to shake up their sexual relationship every now and then and not let sex get so friendly that it never allows for another self to emerge and excite the other person.

The incest taboo is more likely to occur with same-sex couples, where there is not the complementarity of opposite genders. I have had couples tell me that they have become like brothers, or sisters, rather than lovers, that they felt so close that having sex seemed like incest. Neither partner was satisfied with this but they had slipped into a pattern of not having sex and they didn't know how to get out of it.

RITUALIZED SEX

This is a common issue in long-term relationships where much that goes on in a couple's life becomes routine:

> We have sex only on Saturday morning. We always do the same thing in the same place in the same order. We've been doing it this way for years. It's boring but neither of us says anything about it. I guess it's easier this way because nobody has to take responsibility for making it happen any other time. Sometimes we just skip it without talking about it.

TOO MANY DISTRACTIONS

Life is just too crowded with events and obligations—an active social life, professional/business/student commitments, work/school-related problems to think about, organizational responsibilities, family conflicts, save-the-world issues. There just aren't enough hours in the day. Or, it's hard to think about sex with so much on your mind. Or, we're so busy, we just forget to do it.

RELATIONSHIP ISSUES

What starts in other rooms tends to end up in the bedroom—hurt feelings, power struggles, fear of abandonment, resistance to being intimate because of unresolved conflict. Bed is a stage on which many such feelings are likely to be played out, though it is not the venue in which they are usually worked through. Undealt-with anger on the part of one or both partners for instance, is a powerful inhibitor of sexual desire.

SUBSTANCE ABUSE

"I don't want to kiss you when you've been drinking so much. You smell terrible."

"You scare me when you're stoned. You're not yourself. I don't know what you're going to do next."

"I can't communicate with you when you're drunk. You're somewhere else. I don't feel as if I know you. It's a real turnoff."

Two people in different states of being often have a hard time reaching across the chasm to make contact. One may be thinking, "What a prissy, unreasonable kill-joy!" The other may be thinking, "What an inconsiderate, out-of-control jerk!" Not exactly the ideal mind-sets for lovemaking.

REINVENTING SEX IN YOUR RELATIONSHIP

Perhaps *your* sex life is going quite well, thank you. You may then want to skip this section, unless you think there just might be the tiniest chance for improvement.

Sex is arguably the most overhyped issue in the Western world. We're supposed to want it, love it, and be good at it, but we get no training at all for it. Actually, what we do get are the most conflicting messages imaginable. Religious teaching and most families try to steer young people away from sex. It's dirty, dangerous, or sinful. Then, all of a sudden, the young person is an adult and is supposed to be sexually competent and embrace the *joy* of sex. Confusion reigns. And that's only heterosexual confusion.

Gay and lesbian people get an additional message about our sexuality—that it is abnormal, an abomination, and (in some places) unlawful. It's a miracle we can have any sexual satisfaction in our lives at all. But we do, and we have no more problems with our ongoing sexual relationships than the straight folks do, which may not be saying much.

So, when sex wanes, here are some ideas about how to get it to wax again. The idea is to find ways to integrate sex, romance, intimacy, and fun. Romance? When did you last look into your beloved's eyes? I mean really looked directly into those eyes without looking away. When did you last play the old music that used to set the scene for romantic interludes? Isn't it time to do that again, to recapture the mood?

Who initiates? Does the one usually pursuing want to be pursued? Can you boost the volume on your amorous feelings, make the signals louder than usual? Turn the tables on the usual routine, vary the pattern, determine to do something different. Who's responsible for making sex happen? Can you change that?

Have you been shortcutting the foreplay? In too much of a hurry? Slow down. Take your time. Enjoy the sensuality of being with your lover's body. Touch it. Rediscover it. Talk to it. Give yourself permission to do something you've never done before. Surprise your partner. Commit yourself to an erotic adventure. Invite the child in your partner to come out and play with the child in you.

Do adornments turn you on? Put on something you would never ordinarily wear—or that you would certainly never wear right *there*. Let your libido be your guide. Dress crazy. Act crazy. Do anything that's spontaneous (unthinkable?). Make a menu of erotic acts. Order from the menu. Never used sex toys? Maybe it's time to try them. Did that already? Maybe it's time to try some new ones.

If the need is for something more titillating to arouse the lover in you, how about getting out the old erotic videos, magazines, or books on gay or lesbian sex play? (Plenty of all of them around.) Never used erotica before? Why not have this kind of adventure together now? No, you don't have to buy into the values that inspire these enterprises, just use them as props in your own sexual productions. Many lesbians object to the kind of pornography that demeans women. Skip all that. There is now a burgeoning market for lesbian-produced and -oriented erotica for you to experiment with.

If getting back to sex as romance is too difficult to accomplish in your own home setting, how about some trips to romantic places? A client recently told me about making love with his partner on Fire Island in an upstairs bedroom with the windows thrown open and the fog rolling in from the ocean. They had been having a dry spell in their sex life but on this night away from home they felt carried off to a place of incredible sexual intensity.

There are villages and towns everywhere in the world that are perfect backdrops for romantic encounters with your partner. For many people the ocean produces erotic feelings, for others it is the mountains, the desert, snow falling, or the sun blazing. Just getting away from the daily grind can be an aphrodisiac. Is it time *you* journeyed to some off-site playground to reawaken the ardor in your lovemaking?

In addition to the above possibilities for enlivening

your sex life there is always fantasy. I once knew a man whose occupation it was to produce and act out sexual scenarios for the jaded and bored all over the world. These were often spectacular productions with story lines and dialogue, costumes, stunts, simulated life-and-death dramas, all leading to elaborate sex. He used to tell me stories about the incredible lengths people (many of them famous) would go to in order to have unusual erotic experiences. Fantasy can be a powerful (and in his case expensive) stimulus to a lively sex life.

But you don't have to hire a pro. How about your own erotic imagination? Has it been in use lately? Perhaps you've seduced someone in your mind in the not too distant past? Maybe you've engaged in a hot sex fantasy with an imaginary stranger, or even someone you know, but you're too self-conscious to think about it, much less talk about it.

Well, how about a fantasy-a-deux? How about you and your partner cowriting a sexual scenario that stars the two of you? In fantasy you can make anything happen you want. You can each be what you dream of being—or fear becoming. You can do things to each other that you may not be ready to do in reality. You can send messages about something you'd like to be happening that you haven't been able to speak about in real life. You can get down and dirty, be a bawdy, randy version of yourself. Or you can be a "damsel in distress" being rescued by your big, strong male or lesbian lover. The possibilities are endless.

Pat and Paula

Pat and Paula had been together for ten years. While their relationship was loving and affectionate, they had not had sex for the last two years. Both seemed okay with that, until one summer when they went to a women's conference. It seemed as if everywhere they went at the conference they heard talk about lesbian sex. Being on the conservative side, they were a bit embarrassed by all this sex talk.

At night, in their cabin, they wondered aloud what was going on in the lesbian community. When they were younger, lesbians didn't go around describing their sex life. Here, there were public lectures on the anatomy of the vagina, making friends with your clitoris, how to own your orgasm. They saw films on various ways to masturbate, the best buys in vibrators, and understanding sexual response cycles. And none of this was presented with clinical remove. The prevailing tone was "This is all fun. Why don't you try it?"

By the time Pat and Paula left the conference they felt somewhat disoriented, not only because of what they'd seen and heard but because of the sexual stirrings each felt inside. Being rather rusty in the romance department, they weren't quite sure what to do with their feelings. For a while it seemed as if they would return to the old pattern of hugs and kisses but no sex, until Paula resurrected a pamphlet they'd brought home from the conference.

"Your Erotic Imagination Uncensored" consisted of a series of exercises designed to help lesbian couples to be more creative about their sex life. Pat read aloud some of the exercises until Paula stopped her.

"Let's try the sexual fantasy," Paula said precipitously.

Pat looked surprised. "Really?"

"Yes, let's do it right now. Let's each write our own."

Paula got out paper and a pen. The two stared at each other in silence.

Then Pat suddenly said, "I'd like to have one of those dildos you strap to your thigh."

Paula looked startled. "What would you do with it?"

"I'd fuck you until you screamed with ecstasy," Pat answered.

"Okay, I'm screaming and I'm coming, but I want my fingers inside you," Paula said.

"Oh, that feels good, but now I want you to . . ."

Paper and pen forgotten, Pat and Paula were soon deeply into their fantasy, saying things to each other that they had never said before. They giggled, kissed, and hugged, and they put their bodies together and made love. Sex was again part of their life, and continued to be, though it did sometimes take getting into one of their fantasies to trigger the turn-on.

Constructing a fantasy together can lead to serious discussion or to fun and silliness, or it can turn into a lewd and lascivious encounter. The one clear objective in all of this is to return spontaneity to your lovemaking if it *happens* to be at a low ebb. Just making an attempt to do something different may introduce sufficient energy into the old libido to open up whole new vistas in your sex life.

If you are interested in an enriched understanding of your erotic nature and enhancing your sexual skills, here are two books I recommend: *The Lesbian Sex Book* by Wendy Caster and *The New Joy of Gay Sex* by Dr. Charles Silverstein and Felice Picano.

SEXUAL EXCLUSIVITY—WHAT'S BEST?

WHAT WORKS?

Monogamy or nonmonogamy? What is best? What works? What are the considerations? What are the pitfalls? In devising an agreement about sexual exclusivity, how do you construct the most honest and realistic arrangement? Where do you look for guidance—Mom and Pop, friends, gay and lesbian "marriage manuals," gay-oriented movies (scarce, but happening)? Then, once you have an agreement, does it continue to be the right one for you? Does it get checked out periodically to make sure it's still working for both partners?

In twenty-five years of counseling gay and lesbian couples, I have heard about every kind of agreement. I've seen the most unusual agreements work and the most conventional arrangements fall apart. A lot seems to depend on who the people are and what they need most at a given time. More important is the honesty with which agreements are made and maintained.

When arrangements fall apart, it is usually because the parties to them were not honest about what they really wanted or were unable to access their true feelings about their needs. Unfortunately, some arrangements fail because people are just too shy to talk about what they want sexually.

For many people, trust and a feeling of security are most important. These are not the gamblers. They want a monogamous relationship they can rely on, no doubts and fears about what their partner is doing, no anticipation of betrayal and the anguish it usually brings.

For others, arrangements that provide reasonable freedom to have outside sex seem essential to making their relationship work. They don't want to be fenced in.

They want the stability of an ongoing partnership *and* the independence to pursue the sexual fun with others that they enjoyed when they were single. They say the relationship has emotional primacy and that is what really counts.

Needless to say, I am often asked what I think about this hot-button issue. I have, on occasion, vacillated between being politically correct—we should support diversity of thought in our community; we don't need to emulate the heterosexual institution of marriage, which doesn't work very well anyway—and being responsive to what I have seen and what I know from my own experience.

With some exceptions, I believe sexually exclusive partnerships work best for most people. First of all, it isn't a level playing field out there. Even though a couple may have an open relationship, that doesn't mean both partners are having an equally swell time in their pursuit of outside sex. Though they usually deny it, partners do tend to keep score.

Say one is out many nights finding sex in all the right places and the other is at home watching television with the dogs. There will eventually be feelings to deal with—deprivation, envy, resentment. What I have seen most often is that one partner wants the open relationship more than the other, who agrees to it because she or he doesn't want to be thought of as a prude or because sex does sound enticing, but getting out there and doing it is another story.

I have often seen open relationships in which both partners were not *equally* enthusiastic about the idea—accepting, resigned, indifferent, perhaps, but not wholly embracing it. Of course, if the partners do not talk about their feelings, the agreement continues in force as if it were just fine for both, and the resentment of one will probably come out in displaced anger about something else. The remedy here is to review and update the agreement periodically, with both partners being as honest as possible about what their *current* wishes are.

The key to making nonmonogamy work, when it does, seems to be mutually agreeing on the rules and sticking to them. Mattison and McWhirter, in their survey reported in *The Male Couple*, found the following ground rules mentioned most often by nonmonogamous male couples. (Bear in mind that these interviews were done in the late 1970s, when the baths were still open and the potential HIV consequences of multiple-partner unsafe sex were not yet understood.)

These "rules" are not being offered in support of nonmonogamy, only as an example of what some people in open relationships have considered to be important. Conceivably these rules would apply as well to lesbian couples who have agreed not to be monogamous. This is a *collection* of items, not a comprehensive list. None is mutually exclusive.

1. Sex is allowed at places where having a brief sexual interchange is a mutual and unspoken understanding.

2. No sex with mutual friends.

3. Sexual encounters must not interfere with the couple's customary or planned time together.

4. Sex is permissible only when one is out of town.

5. Sexual encounters are always verbally shared with the lover.

6. Talking about it is expected, but it must be at least forty-eight hours after the sex took place.

7. Outside sex is allowed only with advance agreement of one's lover.

8. No emotional involvement with sex partners is allowed.

9. Outside sex is permissible in three-ways or group sex only.

10. Outside sex is permissible, but never discuss it.

11. Outside sex is not permissible at home, or, if it is permitted at home, not while the partner is there alone.

12. Outside sex is permitted at home in the partner's absence, but not in certain places, such as in the couple's bedroom.

13. Secondary emotional relationships with sexual friends are allowed, but the lover is not to be excluded.

And, of course, the indispensable rule now to be added to the list is:

14. All outside sex *must* follow safer sex guidelines.

For some lesbians or gay men who feel they *must* resist the "confinement" of monogamy, what seems to work better than solo sex outside the relationship is sex that involves both partners and one or more others. Three- and four-ways at least give both lovers a chance to enjoy their sexual adventures together. Some say that the stimulation of being with new people is renewing to their own sexual relationship. Philip Blumstein and Pepper Schwartz, in their monumental *American Couples*, had the following to say on the subject:

> Three-ways are often a form of protection. They can take the potential for romance out of sex by creating a less intimate situation. If two people are never alone together, it is easier to ensure that one's partner will not get into emotional trouble.

As important as it is for a couple to decide whether their relationship will be sexually exclusive or not, many have only an unspoken agreement. I often ask clients if they have an agreement about monogamy. They almost always say sure they do. When I ask what it is, one of two things happens. They either clearly articulate the agreement they've made, or they look at one another in a puzzled way as if neither wants to say the wrong thing because they've haven't really discussed it.

I see the haven't-really-discussed-it side more with gay men than with lesbians, probably because casual sexual encounters are much more taken for granted as okay in the gay male than in the lesbian world. Attitudes about this, however, may change drastically when commitment is made to a relationship.

Sometimes the partners discover that each has a quite different idea of what the agreement is—one thinks it's all right to have sex when the other is out of town if it isn't discussed; the other thought they were in agreement about being monogamous all the time.

No, they'd not really talked about it, but each felt certain he knew what the arrangement was. The temptations of nonmonogamy, or even the fantasies about it, seem to have the effect of sometimes dulling even the best of memories.

I have heard many rationales for sex outside the relationship. Often it is about the hunt, which is usually a hunt for personal validation:

"I'm okay because she [or he] found me attractive enough to go to bed with."

The question is, Why is this validation not happening in your relationship with your own lover? Isn't this something that should be addressed and worked on? Or is your notion of being validated still tied to values from the single life—new sexual conquests are the yardstick by which you measure your attractiveness and worth? If that is the case, some serious reevaluating is in order.

There is a kind of affirmation that comes from being with a lover long-term, building a life, growing closer, and finding deeper levels of intimacy and *new* ways to please one another sexually. This person who is your partner finds you attractive enough to spend his or her life with you. What is more validating than that?

If you find yourself continually seeking evidence of your sexual appeal outside your relationship it may be time to look inward to see what is really driving this search. The likelihood is that it has more to do with a long-standing problem with self-esteem than an overactive libido. If that is the case, seeing the hunt for what it is—an effort to fill a void that is about something else entirely—may be the first step in getting a more realistic perspective on the issue of monogamy in your own life.

Another rationale I hear for seeking sex outside the partnership revolves around what I call the "body-type trap":

"I love my partner, but he is just not my body type, so I have to go out occasionally and find that hairy monster/smooth-skinned Adonis/blond, blue-eyed cutie/ dark-haired muscleman I'm turned on by."

Or: "I love my partner, but she is not the slim little blonde/tall and strong butch/dark-haired exotic/soft-bodied earth mother I am really attracted to."

There is obviously no ideal physique or type. There is an *idealized* body image that becomes fixated in one's mind from early exposure to the exemplary bodies seen in magazines and films. Or the idealization can come from one's own fantasies about how one would really like to look, often the exact opposite of how one really does look. Everyone then gets judged by the idealized image.

So what is this person doing with a lover who is not her or his type? What I usually hear is that the ideal type person—the gorgeous hunk or the great-looking babe—is nice to look at but turns out to be not as smart, interesting, and compatible as the incumbent lover.

Recently I was pained to hear Victor, an attractive young man, say he felt like a failure because he didn't have the kind of muscled, gym-toned body that one sees on the streets of West Hollywood. Victor was a successful professional who had no interest in spending time at the gym, but he was in a quandary because his lover, John, was invoking the you're-not-my-body-type rationale for his need to seek outside sex.

As it turned out, John's interest in nonmonogamy was much more about his fear of commitment to a degree of intimacy with Victor that would test emotional skills he wasn't sure he had. When John was able to deal with the basic relationship issue, his need to cruise the streets of West Hollywood became a thing of the past.

The body-type trap is often a smoke screen designed (not necessarily consciously) to avoid looking at personal issues that may feel too hard to handle. When two people cooperate with the I-can't-help-myself scenario that one is presenting, a conspiracy of silence about relationship issues may be in the making. The remedy is to have the courage to get into those issues, not allow a shallow drama about body type to obscure the deeper concerns involved.

Not inconsequential here are the perils that the gay male subculture can present to a relationship. In a long-term partnership one or both people will sometimes need the freedom to be away from the other—spend the evening with a friend. Typically, with gay men, this does not involve visiting the neighborhood bowling alley or playing poker with the guys.

Dinner with a friend might well be in a gay restaurant, perhaps followed by a drink at a gay bar or time spent dancing at a gay club. In all of these environments the air is somewhat charged; the hunt is on for at least some of the people present. This does not mean that a night out will necessarily result in a sexual escapade. People do have control of their behavior. It does mean, however, that temptation is built into these experiences.

It is important for partners to spend time away from one another. When I hear resistance to this on the part of one member of a gay male couple I have learned it is often because that time will be spent where there are wandering eyes and, maybe, wandering lovers. What would help at these times is a frank discussion about this reality and reassurances given about no sexual intentions and agendas.

DEALING (AND NOT DEALING) WITH

HIV-RELATED FEARS

It is hard to imagine how anyone, especially someone in the gay male community, could not have fears about AIDS. If ever a fear was rational and sensible, it is the fear of becoming HIV positive. We all know that HIV disease is preventable, but the enormity of AIDS among us is for some so inhibiting they have trouble being sexual at all. On the other hand, there are those who have come to deal with the danger by defying it. No safer sex for them. They play the odds and *dare* the virus to invade their beings.

This fool's game is usually played under the influence of alcohol or drugs, or out of guilt for having avoided AIDS so far. The game is also played by people who seem unable to connect the cause and effect of unsafe sex and HIV infection (unimaginable but true), or whose lives are so without meaning that being safe doesn't matter. I hope that is not true of anyone reading this book. HIV-related fears have taken a toll on the sex lives of many sero-different male couples, a situation that need not happen.

Hector and Lane

For Hector and Lane life changed dramatically when Hector began to show the first symptoms of AIDS. They had been together five years, and Lane, HIV negative, knew from the beginning that Hector had tested positive. Hector's first opportunistic disease was quickly brought under control, but it felt like a wake-up call to Lane—the first real change of status.

Lanc felt very anxious about what was going to happen to Hector. He was much less in touch with his feelings about himself. He didn't decide consciously that he was going to withdraw from having sex with Hector, he just backed off, shut down, and became unavailable.

Lane and Hector shared a reticence to talk about their relationship, especially the sexual part. As Lane became more inaccessible, Hector assumed that Lane's feelings about him had changed, that Lane no longer loved him or found him attractive. Feeling less attractive to himself because of the illness, Hector feared that Lane would get fed up with the lack of sex in the relationship and would eventually leave him.

When anxiety turned to despair, Hector could no longer remain silent. He insisted that Lane tell him what he was planning to do. Lane was puzzled by the question. What was he planning to do? He wasn't planning to do anything but be with Hector, love him, and take care of him. Hector expressed his surprise. Lane began to get angry.

"How could you think I would be anywhere but here with you? I love you. Why would I go away from you?"

"Well, you obviously don't find me attractive anymore. I feel as if you are running away from me when I want to be sexual with you. I miss our intimacy. Don't you?"

Lane looked uncomfortable. "Of course I miss it, but I've just been kind of into myself lately."

"What does that mean, *into yourself*?"

"You know, just not feeling like being involved sexually."

Hector felt stopped by Lane's comments, but he was in this now, and he knew he had to go ahead. "Okay, let's talk about *it*."

" 'It'—what's 'it'?"

"My HIV status, my falling T-cell count, my infection, my illness, my AIDS."

"Oh, come on, Hector. What's that got to do with it?"

Hector stared incredulously at Lane. He began to realize what was happening—Lane was frightened about becoming infected, and he was denying it to himself.

"Lane, are you afraid I'll infect you? Is that why you have stopped having sex with me?"

Lane looked chagrined. His eyes filled with tears. "Sweetheart, I didn't want to hurt your feelings. I didn't want to talk about this at all."

"But don't you see, Lane, my feelings are already hurt. They're devastated. With you not telling me the truth, I fill the void with terrible thoughts of rejection and abandonment."

"It's so hard to talk about."

"I know, but we have to talk about it."

"I'm embarrassed. I do have some fear that I'll get infected, too. That's why I've been so . . . unresponsive. I'm afraid."

"Listen, it feels so much better to know what's happening. I certainly don't want you to get infected. There's plenty of information around about safer sex. I just want to feel you close again."

"Me, too," Lane said. "It feels so much better to say it out loud. I *am* afraid. I've been so guilty because I knew it must be hurting you. I was just stuck there."

"Well, I'm afraid, too, about a dozen different things. I guess we need to keep talking about this."

Lane smiled. "We need to talk about it—and *do* something about it."

Two things are illustrated in Hector and Lane's story. First, the importance of talking about whatever fears either partner has. The focus is on reality when that happens. If the HIV-negative partner keeps quiet about his fears of being infected his partner may well decide he is being rejected because he is no longer attractive. Who needs that kind of blow to the ego while struggling with the effects of illness?

Fearing infection is natural, normal, and understandable. Coping with rejection in the absence of information as to what it's about can be painful. That kind of pain *can* be avoided. The virus is a stealthy intruder. Don't let it invade your relationship any more than is necessary. Staying open about feelings is one way to control the emotional effects of coping with HIV and AIDS.

Second, there *is* something to be grieved. If you and your partner feel anger or sadness at not being able to do the sexually exciting things you did before, you may need to mourn that loss together. Speak frankly about how you miss the old sexual activities and the freedom to jump into them any time you were aroused.

Having mourned the loss of what you can't do anymore can free you to set about discovering new sexual options. The bottom line here is summed up in a slogan of the safer-sex movement: *"The virus is spread by certain sexual acts; the virus is not produced by sex."*

It is tempting to present here a listing of sexual activities that are, and are not, risky for transmitting HIV, but I would be on shaky ground since I have seen the list change from year to year and I know that change will continue as research yields more precise knowledge about how transmission occurs.

Certainly the proper use of condoms is, and will probably remain, high on the list of ways to reduce the possibility of transmission. Mutual masturbation affords the sharing of a sexual experience without the exchange of bodily fluids. And, to be safer than safe, there are various forms of degenitalized sexual contact that can have the effect of awakening the senses and gratifying the need to be touched and wanted: massage, caressing, holding, back rubs, kissing.

While most of these ideas can apply to women as well as to men, lesbian couples are much less at risk for transmission of HIV unless one or both lovers are IV drug users who have shared needles or have had sexual contact with HIV-infected male partners. If there is any possibility of a partner's being infected, the use of dental dams is recommended by many experts, and safer sex guidelines should be followed.

In relationships where both partners are HIV-positive safer sex is also recommended by the experts, who warn that there are realistic reasons for sero-positive couples to be cautious. We now know that there are many different strains of the virus, and adding a new strain to the mix may accelerate the disease process.

Some HIV strains are more virulent than others. Infection by other viruses (hepatitis B, for instance) may further weaken an already compromised immune system. On the surface it may seem like "What's the difference? We're both HIV-positive already." The difference may be in a long period of good health or one that is foreshortened. Of course, your physician is the best resource for information about all of this.

Once informed about safer sex options, negotiating with your partner about what, when, and how is the next step. HIV fears may have interrupted your sex life, but that does not have to mean that fear wins. If an open and honest approach to reorganizing your sex life is followed, there is every reason to believe that erotic adventure can again become part of your loving relationship.

THE OTHER VOICE OF SEX

There are many reasons people might forgo sex in their relationship. On a temporary basis, the illness or depression of one of the partners could inhibit the desire of that person to be sexual. Unexpressed anger can make it almost impossible to want to share intimacy until the feelings are worked through.

More profound are the conflicts sometimes generated by internalized homophobia—someone may not be sure if being gay or lesbian is really okay, and the whole issue doesn't have to be confronted if there is no sex. We'll never know many truly homosexual relationships are not consummated because of self-denial.

But we are more concerned here with two people forgoing sex for reasons that are not pathological or

homophobic. They just find that their relationship has
come to work better if their sexual contact is nongenital,
what I would call "the other voice of sex." Maybe it's
matching low libidinal levels, maybe it's lassitude, maybe
it's just lack of interest. It doesn't matter as long as both
parties are in agreement about it.

We are so oversold on the importance of sex to bonding, nurturing, and being validated that some gay and
lesbian people have the misguided notion that their relationship is over if they are not having sex with their partner. A reasoned examination of this development may be
in order, but concluding that an intimate partnership
cannot succeed without sex on a regular basis is unin-
formed and naive.

This point is supported by the findings of the 1994
University of Chicago study, *Sex in America: A Definitive
Survey*. From interviews with 3,432 scientifically selected
respondents, the authors, Robert T. Michael, John H.
Gagnon, Edward O. Laumann, and Gina Kolata, con-
cluded that:

> The general picture of sex with a partner in America
> shows that Americans do not have a secret life of abun-
> dant sex. If nothing else, the startlingly modest amounts
> of partnered sex reveal how much we as a society can de-
> ceive ourselves about other people's sex lives.

There are many couples who have evolved ways to
bond and to nurture one another without benefit of pro-
ducing each other's orgasms. As long as both partners
know for sure that what is happening is mutually okay, it
is an act of love to respect the other's wish not to be
forced into unwanted genital sex.

"The other voice of sex"—the nongenital voice—may
involve various kinds of body contact quite satisfying to

these partners: hugging, holding, snuggling, and caressing. Exploring your partner's body, acknowledging changes, appreciating its contours, loving its presence, is sexual in its essence. Mouth kissing is making contact at the body's most powerful (and most vulnerable) point of entry. Massage nurtures the senses. Sharing a life strengthens the bond as no other activity could; choosing to be with this person over anyone else can be validation far beyond any momentary triumph of the libido.

In another sense, friendship is the bonus of intimate partnership. For many, if not most, it is the real prize that emotional attachment to another human being bestows. To know that someone understands you, is interested in what is happening to you, and is there on a daily basis is to know the reassurance of intimate friendship. That precious spin-off of partnership can happen with or without a genital sex component to the relationship.

The other voice of sex may sing just as sweetly to you, though sometimes doubts filter in because of those wonderful people who always have an opinion about how other people should be living their lives.

Sarah and Pat

Sarah and Pat had shared a life for thirty years. They were both successful in their professions and gave a considerable amount of time to organizations in the lesbian community. Their social life consisted mainly of parties and dinners with other women also active in the community. As far as Pat and Sarah were concerned, they had a pretty good life. In their fifties, they had been together since they met in college. They seldom were in conflict and were consistently affectionate with one another.

One night Sarah and Pat attended a meeting of the

board members of various lesbian organizations. Many of those present were young women. The session focused on how different lesbian organizations could be more cooperative with one another. Eventually the evening segued into an informal social event. Sarah and Pat enjoyed talking to the younger women and invited two of the couples—Marti and Sean, Abby and Robin—to dinner the following week. The older couple was delighted at the prospect of an evening with their younger sisters.

On the night of the dinner party, everyone seemed to be having a good time. After a few glasses of wine, the conversation began to shift slowly from generalities to a specific topic: sex. Sarah and Pat tried not to show how shocked they were. Marti, one of the more assertive young women, sat forward in her chair and asked, quite calmly, "Now, Pat and Sarah, tell us, how often do you have sex?"

The room fell silent as all heads turned to the two older women, both of whom looked as startled as if they had just been told they were under arrest for murder. Pat managed a small laugh. "Now, c'mon. Is that an appropriate question to ask someone you don't know very well?"

The young women looked at one another and then in unison their heads all nodded yes. Abby said, "Aren't you supposed to be role models for us? Sex is important in our lives. We don't usually have this kind of opportunity to get information from someone older whom we respect."

Sean said, "We know this is a little sudden, but we decided on the way over here to ask you because we talk about it among ourselves, but it would really be helpful to know about you."

Sarah took a deep breath and said, "Look, we're just

not used to talking about this with people we don't know, so I think we have to decline an answer."

After another slightly tense hour of conversation the young women left. Sarah and Pat fell into chairs, sat silent for a minute, and then both spoke at once.

"Can you believe it?"

Sarah shook her head. "I don't exactly feel old in my life, but tonight . . ."

"Tell me about it. Do you think they did that just to shock us?"

"Well, if they did, they succeeded."

Pat said, "I was so glad when you said we didn't wish to discuss it. I mean . . . how would we have answered that question even if we wanted to?"

Sarah stared at her partner. "Do you mean that we should be embarrassed to say that we don't have sex, at least not the kind they're probably talking about?"

"I'd be uncomfortable with that answer, wouldn't you?"

Sarah thought for a while. "Yes, I would, too, but I'm thinking about why . . . why we have to be embarrassed about something that is nobody's business but ours."

Pat said, "The real question is why do we have to be embarrassed at all? Do we think we're doing something wrong? Aren't we living in the way we want to live?"

"Absolutely. We don't talk about it every day, but I think we are in agreement, aren't we?"

"I'm happy with the way our life is," Pat said, "but maybe we *should* be talking about it."

"I guess we are right now. I love our life. I wouldn't change anything about it, and I certainly wouldn't change anything because these young lesbians might be implying that we are doing something wrong." Sarah's voice had an edge of anger to it.

"I don't think they were implying that. I think they were just asking a question."

"So why are we so defensive about this sexual issue? Do *we* think we're doing it wrong?"

"Sounds like it, doesn't it? You know what I think we should do? I think we should meet with those young people, tell them the truth, and try to teach them something."

"Like what?" Sarah asked.

"Like how important it is to make choices that fit your own life, not someone else's ideas about what your life should be."

"Sounds familiar, doesn't it?"

Pat laughed. "You mean all those relatives who like to tell us that we are living a sin because we're different from them?"

"Exactly."

Sarah and Pat sat in silence for a minute. Pat spoke in a quiet voice. "This is going to take some guts, you know. Sounds a little pompous. Who appointed us to teach them the lessons of life?"

"They did, remember? They reminded us that we are their role models."

"Well, are you up to this?"

"I am if you are."

In the next week Sarah called the two couples and asked them to come to lunch on the weekend. Having been told by Sarah "We're ready to answer your question now," the four young women eagerly accepted the invitation.

On arrival, Marti was carrying a large book graphically illustrating a variety of lesbian sex acts. She said, "We thought this might help us talk about specifics, if you want to get into anything like that."

After lunch the group settled into the living room and Pat began.

"We've thought it over and decided that your question was not as unanswerable as it seemed to us the other night. The fact is, we do have a very passionate connection, Sarah and I. We have a lot of body contact, and we are quite affectionate with each other."

Pat picked up the book and began turning the pages.

"We just don't do any of the things that are in this book."

The young women looked puzzled. Robin asked, "What do you mean? If you don't do what's in this book, you mean you don't have sex."

Sarah answered, "What makes you think the only ways to have sex are the ones shown in this book?"

No one spoke until Marti said, "Okay, tell us. That's what we're here for."

Sarah said, "No, I think you're here to have *your* notions of lesbian sexuality validated. We are trying to tell you that the kind of genital sex in this book is not what we do. We have chosen to show our love to each other by being intimate in many ways, but not including [back to the book] these sex acts. That is our mutual choice. We're both happy with it."

"But . . . that means you don't have sex at all," Sean said.

"Wrong," Pat answered. "Our intimacy is very fulfilling. We have a strong emotional bond, and we express it physically. We cherish each other's bodies. You asked how often we have sex? Our erotic connection is there all the time."

The group sat in silence.

Sarah asked, "Well, what do you think? Have we answered your question?"

Abby said, "I think you have, but I'm not sure how that relates to us."

Pat answered, "What we really want to convey to you is how important it is to make up your own mind about how you want to live your life. If it's different from what others do, even the majority, it doesn't matter. You matter. You owe it to yourself to do what feels best to you, as long as both of you in your relationship are okay with it."

Marti said, "And if we decide that we want to be sexual like this?" She raised the book, open to an illustration of two women in orgasmic ecstasy.

Pat laughed. "We don't judge you for doing what feels best to you, and you don't judge us for doing what feels best to us. That's the whole idea."

Can a gay or lesbian relationship be intimate and fulfilling without sex? You might not think so from reading much that I have written in this chapter, but the fact is, many men and women have ongoing, committed, passionately devoted emotional attachments to one another that do not include genital sex at all. Sarah and Pat obliged by being candid with their young friends. The truth is, as long as both partners are satisfied with expressing their love on their own terms, it is nobody's business but their own.

CHAPTER 7

The Challenge to Keep Growing— Does It Have to Be So Much Work?

I had initially seen Bill and his lover, Martin, as a couple. Now it was several months since Martin had died and Bill sat alone in my office. He was talking about how much he missed his lover, how precious their time together had been.

"If only I could hold him again, just feel his body next to mine, kiss his face. I would give anything to have those moments back."

Bill's eyes filled with tears. "We don't appreciate enough what we have, what we take for granted, until we don't have it anymore. If only more lovers would cherish all of their time together, because when it's gone, it is so irretrievably gone."

I, too, teared up then, thinking about Martin and thinking about my own relationship and the times I am only partially present with my lover, preoccupied with the minutiae of life and the challenges of my own projects. I silently vowed to heed Bill's words—to be more fully present with my partner, to value our moments and not take them for granted.

I kept my vow for a time, then slipped back into my old ways. I see now I have to renew that vow and do so again and again, reminding myself how precious the gift of intimacy is and how alert one must be to its nurturance. This is not always easy to do, but it is the essential task of keeping our relationships vital as well as permanent.

The challenge to grow is implicit in every intimate partnership. In competition with this is the resistance to growing—the inclination to hold on to the status quo, to reject change, to preserve what is familiar as a hedge against whatever unknown challenges the future might bring. It is tempting to resist change. You feel safer doing so because you already know your life, your relationship, what's expected of you, what you're capable of. There is comfort in predictability.

The reality is that, like it or not, our lives and our needs evolve. Our sense of who we are expands or contracts, and the people close to us are affected by our changes. Sometimes love must be redefined to fit whatever new contours to our lives have emerged. This usually takes work.

Too often I hear:

"I'm tired of trying. This is just too hard."
"If a relationship is this much work it can't be right."
"Oh, so now I have to walk on eggshells, always say the right thing. I don't want to live this way."

Relationships are intricate and complex and require ongoing maintenance, just as the people in them require continuous attention to their changing needs. Those who are complaining about their relationships' being too much work are often those who believe in the myth that love conquers all—that two people's being "in love" is a sufficient condition to overcome any problem.

It simply isn't true. Love may be the glue that holds a union together when the going gets rough. It may be what sweetens the reconciliation when the problems are resolved. But it is the willingness to engage in dialogue and the skill to work through conflict that really make for relationship success.

THE INITIAL PROBLEM—

OUR IMPERFECT PARTNERS

So now we have this partner who is *it*—the one who has taken on the responsibility of understanding, loving, and taking care of us, the one we have come to depend on, and the one who will surely fail us at times, just as our imperfect parents did.

Try as we may to effect a change, hoping against hope for transformation, the imperfect partner with whom we find ourselves paired remains flawed—exhibiting blind spots, emotional quirks, misguided thinking, and an inability to appreciate our superior wisdom and know-how.

Why do we so routinely find ourselves in relationships with these imperfect partners? Because that's the only kind there is. We are all imperfect partners, flawed and inconsistent, often too self-absorbed, and capable of inflicting injury on those we love, inadvertently and otherwise.

Against the backdrop of our *illusions* about relationships, a partner's imperfections can stand out in luminous detail. For instance, if you have a lover who is smart and strong and caring you would expect that person to exhibit those traits all the time. So, when your lover gives in to weakness and behaves stupidly and insensitively, you wonder what happened. Does this mean you can no longer depend on this person, or have you just lost the illusion that he or she will be your Rock of Gibraltar all the time?

The loss of faith in a partner's infallibility is, in a sense, loss of the fantasy that at last you have found someone to take care of you in the way your parents did (if you come from a functional family) or didn't (if yours was one of the ubiquitous dysfunctionals).

The disappointment that attends your lover's failure to behave reasonably and compassionately toward you may tap into feelings you have toward the people who were inconsistently there for you early in your life, when reliability and dependability counted the most.

"Oh, I've got that all worked out," says my client, denying that her anger toward her mother for being critical has anything to do with her resentment toward her partner, who is actually just trying to give some constructive advice.

None of us is immune to the irrationality of projecting onto an imperfect lover the culpability of an imperfect parent. The task is to sort out the inequities of the past from the failed expectations of the present. I don't assume that you have not done this kind of work already, but I find it is not always easy to hold on to such connections even after they are made.

We all like to think that we are grown-up and sophisticated enough to live in the present and not let long-ago family scenarios intrude upon our contemporary lives. We move on from childhood, but that needy little kid inside moves right on with us.

CRITICISM RECONSIDERED

In the twenty-five years I've been working with gay and lesbian couples, I have heard just about every complaint imaginable. One I hear a lot is "I'm tired of being criticized."

There are those among us who deal with our discomfort over a partner's imperfections by being critical. The criticism doesn't even have to be direct. It can be subtle and implied, but the message gets through anyway: "You're doing it wrong again."

Criticism hurts; it pares away at a person's sense of self-esteem; it may create rifts in the loving connection you have with your partner. Being critical can be a strategy for not dealing with issues that are too threatening. It may be easy for me to criticize you. It may not be so easy for me to tell you that I envy and resent your good looks because I doubt my own attractiveness.

I think criticism should always be reconsidered. Here's a way to do that. Ask yourself these questions the next time you feel the need to start criticizing your partner.

- "Could this just be about how different we are and how uncomfortable that is for me?"
- "Aside from wanting to be 'helpful,' what else might be going on with me? Could I possibly be envious or competitive?"
- "Could I be doing what I've picked up from my own parent even though I hated that criticizing behavior?"
- "Am I wanting to be hurtful because I am angry about something I'm not ready to deal with?"

Exploring your own hidden agendas can be very revealing. I recently discovered a hidden agenda of my own in this way. I had been on a week-long binge of criticizing my partner. When I asked myself what I was doing, I discovered that I was really acting out resentment I felt because of the rapid pace of her career at a time when my own seemed to be moving in slow motion.

While my partner went to business every day, interacting with many people and being stimulated by all kinds of challenges, I sat at home writing, alone. Even though I had carefully arranged my isolation so I *could* write, I felt lonely, deprived, envious, and resentful.

I couldn't express these feelings directly, of course, because they were not *rational*. It was not her fault that I spent my days alone with only three little Yorkies to talk to or that Molly, Minnie, and Max were more interested in sleeping or getting their dinner than they were in my lonely feelings. None of this was her fault, but she became the target of my resentment nevertheless.

It took a tough confrontation with myself to realize what I was doing—that the criticism of her grew out of my need to puncture her balloon. I knew I had to talk about this with her. I had to confess to feelings I didn't admire. I had to let her in on my need to spoil her good feelings, and listen to her annoyed reaction, her irritation with me. It was a tough trip.

Though it was an invaluable experience, there were times during this discussion when I wanted to just turn it off, to flee, to be somewhere else. I stuck it out because I knew I couldn't really run away from the feelings; they would stay with me until they were properly dealt with. We ended up with a better understanding of what was happening to each of us. We could feel close again, no unexpressed anger between us, ready to return to the relaxed fit of our relationship.

No matter how raw an experience confrontation is in the moment, or how vulnerable it makes you feel, it is crucial to stay with it until you feel the anger subside and the defensiveness fall away. Only then are you free enough to hear accurately what the other is saying and to accept responsibility for whatever your own contribution to the problem might be. Only then can trust be restored.

FEAR OF DIFFERENCES

If your need to be critical of your partner is a function of how different the two of you are, think about why the differences are troubling. I think it's a little scary at times to realize that you have tied your fate to a person who may not think, feel, or act as you do, most of the time.

Could you be hurt inadvertently because this person doesn't "get" you in all your complexities? Could you do the same to your partner? Of course, but it is *in* the differences—and the continuing effort to understand and accept them—that the texture of the relationship is elaborated.

Fear of differences forms the basis for racism, homophobia, and every kind of unjust discrimination. We put people down who have differences that scare us. That's how we neutralize the fear, by making them inferior to us. The same thing can happen with a lover. We are threatened by the differences we see. We criticize as a way of disempowering that person.

What is the remedy for this misguided tactic? I believe it is to go inside yourself and find out what is really going on. Could this be about your own doubts and fears as a person? Do you need a companion who validates your every thought and emotion and action? Do you need that mirror to look into to know that you are okay, or can you let your lover be different enough from you to tolerate some unpredictability?

BECOMING THE CRITICAL PARENT

Perhaps you had a parent who was always criticizing. It is disconcerting indeed that we pick up from our parents behaviors that we disapprove of and reject.

We feel we can't help ourselves. There you are being critical again, just as your mother or father was, and you can't believe you are doing this. It is behavior you saw and absorbed at an impressionable age; it is a way of being in the world that made its mark on you and it isn't easy to get rid of.

I had a mother who covered her own self-doubts by being critical of others, including me. I found that behavior appalling when I became old enough to see it for what it was. Do I have a tendency to be critical of my partner? Yes, but I monitor that tendency because I know where it comes from. I also know that I am a mature adult and I can design my own interactions with people. I am not stuck with what I learned in my family.

I am responsible for what I do in my relationships, and therefore I can choose responses that I feel good about, that fit with my perception of who I am. Yes, sometimes I slip, I become my mother, I criticize unnecessarily, but I usually know what I'm doing and why. Awareness is instrumental to behavior change. I'm working on it. I probably always will be.

UNSPOKEN CRITICISM

This is about those critical thoughts you have about your partner that you don't give voice to because you don't want to be seen as someone who is constantly criticizing.

So what do you do? You engage in a running dialogue with yourself. You flood yourself with messages about how inconsiderate, shortsighted, stubborn, or (fill in the blank) your partner is.

"She is so damned insensitive."
"He is so self-centered he can't think of anyone else."
"There she goes again telling me what to do."
"He's just like his mother, bitching all the time."

The result is that you talk yourself into feeling alienated from the person. You become distant and cool.

Since these messages cannot be accessed by your partner there is some mystery about what is going on. Only you can stem the tide of this silent diatribe that is so noisy in your head. You can start by posing questions such as these to yourself:

"Why am I doing this?"
"What is the purpose of my running these thoughts in my head?"
"What effect is this having on how I feel about my partner?"
"What is this doing to my relationship?"

I think we get into the negative interior monologue as a way of protecting ourselves from the unknown consequences of allowing critical thoughts to be dealt with openly.

Sometimes it may be better to shut off the monologue, just stop the flow of words, counter them with thoughts about the good things your partner has done for you. You do have control over the messages you give *yourself,* which in turn shapes how you feel toward your partner and what is going to happen between you.

INSTRUCTIVE VERSUS DESTRUCTIVE CRITICISM

There is one kind of criticism that *instructs* the other person about some change you would like, and there is another kind that *destroys* the probability that constructive change will occur at all. The kind that instructs is offered from the point of view of someone experiencing dissatisfaction. It's an "I" message that describes a personal reaction.

Destructive criticism is an attack on the other person. It's a "you" message that disparages or pathologizes the individual, who must then defend against the attack. There is little chance that anything positive will come out of this transaction.

Let's say your partner drives faster than you would like. You are not only scared but angry:

"You are driving like a maniac!"
"You're homicidal. You're trying to kill me, aren't you?"
"Are you crazy? This is not the Indianapolis Speedway!"

This driver is most likely now in either a defensive or a counterattack mode. How different it would be if the presentation was as follows:

"*I* feel frightened when you drive so fast. Would you slow it down for me, please?"

This is less about criticizing and more about what *you* are experiencing. Put this way, your partner can more easily hear what you are saying. Taking a few seconds to switch gears in order to put the focus on yourself gives the other person options for responding and less reason to defensively reject what you have to say.

Natasha and Janet

Here are two versions of a critical encounter between long-time partners. These two women are in the midst of remodeling their home. The work is disruptive and going more slowly than they had anticipated. Each is blaming the other for the delay.

> *Natasha: "I don't know why you had to change the plans at the last minute. Now we'll be living in half our house for an extra two weeks. What you want is the only thing that matters to you. You just don't care about me."*
>
> *Janet: "I was only trying to have the best result possible. You are the one who is inconsiderate. You seem to care only about comfort. You just want your way. You are impossible!"*
>
> *Natasha: "You are the one who is impossible. You're doing this for yourself, because you want those extra closets. You just bully your way through to get what you want and then pretend you did it for me."*
>
> *Janet: "It seems to give you pleasure to put me down. What a mean person you can be. All you care about is criticizing me!"*

Let's rewrite Natasha's and Janet's encounter replacing "you" with "I" messages.

> *Natasha: "I'm really feeling disrupted having to live in half our house for another two weeks. I was looking forward to being finished with this remodeling."*
>
> *Janet: "I guess I did get focused on the additional plans, but when you seem to care more about being comfortable than having the best result I begin to feel impatient with you."*
>
> *Natasha: "I'm also irritated. I don't like that feeling. Living in this mess is hard enough without having to be angry with you, too."*

Janet: "I just wanted to please you with the extra closet space. I don't like feeling criticized when I was just trying to do something nice for you."

Natasha: "Okay, but I want you to hear that it's important to me to have something to say about what goes into my own house. I want to be consulted."

If only we could rewrite our encounters like this, replacing critical, hurtful words with gentler language. Instructive criticism conveys information without challenging anyone's intentions or mounting an attack on your partner's integrity.

One last thought about being critical. Think about the messages we've been getting all of our gay and lesbian lives:

"You're doing it wrong."

"What you are is wrong."

Haven't we had enough of that? I think we owe it to one another *not* to reinforce the message—"You're doing it wrong"—by criticizing each other's feelings, thoughts, and behavior with the ease that we sometimes do. *Society* makes it tough on us. Let's not make it even tougher on ourselves. We can be just as strong in our love as anyone else, but we can be just as vulnerable to being hurt, too, maybe more so.

DO I REALLY HAVE TO LIKE THIS
PERSON ALL THE TIME?

I love my partner. I treasure her talents, her generosity, her heartfelt caring, and her presence in my life. Do

I *like* her all the time? Frankly, no. Sometimes I don't like her much at all. At those times, I find her habits annoying and her approach to life off-putting.

For instance, I can't stand her tendency to do things at the last minute, and it's especially irritating when what she is doing turns out just fine. Her sense of humor is variously killer cynical or theater of the absurd. She shows me cartoons that she thinks are riotous that I don't even get.

When I open the door to her office at home and see the stacks of books, piles of files, overflowing boxes of magazines and papers, every surface in the room sprouting disorder (or so it seems to me), I feel immobilized. I want to bring order to the chaos, but I cannot; it's not mine to control. I am powerless to affect this universe of hers in which she claims she knows exactly where everything is, and often enough she does.

Then there is her largesse with food. When she shops she buys not one of each item but often a whole case. When I point out that there is no more room in our cupboards, she scoffs and somehow manages to pack her purchases in anyway. My eyes glaze over as I open a kitchen cabinet and immediately have to give up on finding what I'm looking for because it is hidden (I assume) behind jars, bottles, and cartons of enough food to feed an army. I am frustrated. I am irritated.

These may not seem like serious offenses, but when order and planning are central to one's functioning, as they are to mine, disorder is chaos in the brain and last-minute planning feels like life out of control. Of course, I realize that the disparity in our habits is as much my problem as hers, possibly more. And that is the point I want to make here. Just because she is different from me she is not an inferior human being, or unworthy of my respect, or ineligible to be my loving partner.

I have clients who object to aspects of their partners' way of being in the world. They don't like certain behaviors or attitudes, therefore they conclude that they don't like the *person* and they are in the wrong relationship. Having decided this, they are ready to bail out in order to find someone with whom they can have the *right relationship*.

I don't like certain things about my partner, but I don't conclude that I am in the wrong relationship. I'm quite sure there are things about me that my partner doesn't like and would rather not have to live with. I do have an obsessive need to be orderly; I do nag about planning; I am not the most flexible person around. We tolerate each other's differences, sometimes more easily than at other times. But *mainly* we value and admire each other and love our life together.

It is the rare couple who never have lapses in the affection and admiration they feel for one another. Such lapses are part of the emotional texture of a relationship. Only if you have been able to find a mirror image of yourself would there not be differences that irritate and annoy. But even with a mirror image you could have problems. If you didn't like yourself very much you probably wouldn't like the person who reflects you back to yourself.

No, you don't have to like the person you're with all the time. Just don't let temporary lapses in affection create doubts about the viability of the relationship. Instead, think about this: we can sometimes get so invested in proving we're right that we forgo the possibility that two people, doing things differently, can both be right.

Carol and Tina

These two women came to me in a state of agitation. Together for eight years, they said they had decided to part and wanted help with making it a fair and equitable breakup. It didn't take long to determine that neither woman really wanted to break up. The problem seemed to be that they "argued" too much. When I asked what they usually argued about the answer came from both, in unison: "She always has to be right!"

The tale I was told was one of disagreements that became mired in the quicksand of *keeping the record straight*:

Carol: "*I distinctly remember you saying that you didn't want to go to that party. Why else would I have gone alone?*"

Tina: "*I said no such thing. I merely questioned why we would want to go to a party given by someone we don't even like.*"

Carol: "*That is absolutely not true. You said, 'I don't want to go to this party. I don't like that woman.'*"

Tina: "*Oh, I didn't say that at all. And I certainly didn't suggest you go without me.*"

Carol: "*You just don't want to remember it the way it happened. You said to me, 'Go if you want to, but I'm not interested.' So I went.*"

Tina: "*Never. Never would I tell you to go to a party without me. You are just wrong about all of this. I know what I said and that is why I know you're wrong.*"

Carol: "*Well, I know what I said, too, and you definitely said, 'Go if you want.'*"

Tina: "*No, I didn't.*"

The conclusion that Tina and Carol came to was that they really didn't like one another because why else would they disagree so much, and if they didn't like each other they shouldn't be together. I asked them to tell me what their life was like when they weren't disagreeing. Immediately subdued, they said they had a lot in common and usually enjoyed the same things.

"Why, then, do you want to break up?" I asked.

Tina answered, "I don't think she likes me. She argues with everything I say. She always has to be right. I'm too frustrated."

Carol said, "I have a very good memory and I remember exactly what I have said. She distorts my words. It's true, I don't like her when she does that."

I pointed out that not liking some piece of behavior does not necessarily mean you don't like the person, and it certainly isn't a basis for upending your whole life. I gave my lecture on our memories' being subject to the impact of new experiences that can subtly change the data around. I posed the question of how much each one's need to be right was influencing the manner in which her memories were retrieved and reconstructed.

Carol began to talk about how she felt disoriented when Tina would deny something Carol remembered her saying: "I have to defend myself in order to maintain my sanity. I know that sounds extreme, but it is really the way I feel. I have to keep the record straight in order to remind myself that I'm not crazy."

I asked Carol if there was any possibility that she might have misunderstood Tina but then had to take a stand on what she thought she heard to defend her honor. Carol hesitated before she nodded her head and said, "I guess that's possible."

I asked Tina if she thought she might be doing the same thing. She shrugged her shoulders. "Maybe."

We talked about how easy it is to lose your perspective when you are so *mobilized* to prove that *you* are the one who is right. People get into this mind-set for different reasons. Sometimes it might be a battle with parents (who were always right) that is still going on in one's head.

At other times it might be a tactic to avoid letting a

partner in closer, a way of controlling the content of encounters and keeping them safe and familiar. An argument about whose memory was more accurate can be depended on to take up time and energy. Intimacy issues easily take a backseat to discord.

Eventually Tina and Carol were able to see that the behavior they didn't like in one another could, with understanding and work, be altered, that it was the behavior and not the person they disliked. With this perspective they decided that being together was infinitely better than breaking up.

I have seen too many gay and lesbian couples give up on their relationships because they didn't understand, or chose to ignore, the important distinction between not liking certain things about a partner and deciding this was the wrong relationship for them.

Behavior can be changed, but there must be a willingness to address the hard issues, to do the work. Presumably you want to have a partnership that endures. That means one that can withstand some stormy days and nights, that no one is going to run away because of a patch of turbulence. It also means you may have to stretch, to reach beyond your own limits, to open up to another's imperfections as well as to your own. That is what growth in relationship is all about.

AVOIDING CONFLICT—

THE BOOMERANG EFFECT

An important part of the challenge to keep growing concerns how a couple deals with the tensions that occur in every loving partnership. When two people have been together for a while there is often a dilemma about how to deal with patterns of behavior that get one's ire up but aren't quite disturbing enough to justify a painful confrontation. You convince yourself that you can live with this annoyance because there is so much in the relationship that is right and good.

The longer one puts off dealing with frustrations, the tougher it gets to talk about them. When time has gone by, and your dissatisfaction has never been brought up, an ensuing spontaneous explosion of anger can feel to the other person like an attack coming out of nowhere, unprovoked and undeserved.

Here we are at the core of the dilemma: what is more important at any given time—peace and harmony at all costs or taking the risk of antagonizing a partner in an effort to make the relationship work better for both of you?

In a sense this is about focusing on the present versus focusing on the future of the partnership. If only the present matters, the status quo is most important: don't rock the boat, keep it pleasant, avoid conflict.

If the future matters at least as much as the present, deal with the issues, be willing to push through denial and incur anger, persist in your mission—because your motivation is of the highest order: you are trying, at some risk, to improve the most important relationship in your life. You are not doing this to be hurtful but to bring a greater degree of authenticity to your dealings with one another.

The following story illustrates the boomerang effect avoiding conflict can have.

Lane and Gerald

Lane and Gerald both came from families that were somewhat volatile, causing each to vow that in his own adult relationships conflict would be held to a minimum. They cooperated to make this possible by agreeing that any time one got steamed up about something he would leave and not come back until the feelings had subsided and they could talk calmly about the problem.

In fact, by the time they got back together each of these times, the discussion was usually benign enough to be beside the point because each tended to tell himself in the interim that nothing was worth a fight. They had gone on like this for several years. It was a big surprise, therefore, when Lane one day confronted Gerald with such vehemence that both were in a state of shock.

Lane thought he had, for the most part, grown accustomed to Gerald's tendency to leave his clothes, his papers, and the contents of his pockets everywhere in the house, but on this day, while cleaning up for guests arriving very shortly, Lane discovered the living room littered with saved-up old magazines and newspapers that Gerald had been cutting recipes from.

Clippings were everywhere. Magazines were tossed randomly about, some fallen open to where pages had been torn out. Obviously, Gerald had started this project the night before, abandoned it when he was too tired to go on, and forgotten it was there.

Lane stood looking at the disarray and suddenly he felt overwhelmed with anger.

"God damn it, Gerald! What is this mess? I'm sick of cleaning up your messes. You have no consideration for anyone but yourself. Get in here!"

Gerald peered cautiously around the doorway.

"What?"

"I'll tell you what. Don't you ever think of the consequences of your behavior? You just use our house like a garbage dump. I live here, too, you know."

"Lane, what is the problem? Just pick up the stuff and put it in the bedroom."

"This is *really* outrageous! Who do you think you are? I'm not your servant. Pick up your own goddamn stuff."

"I think you should go for a walk."

Glaring at Gerald, Lane shouted, "What you need is some self-discipline, and if you don't get it together I *am* out of here!"

"Fine. Go ahead. I don't like being shouted at. I don't need this!"

Lane went out the front door and slammed it behind him. Gerald stood looking at the door, shaken and disbelieving that this could have happened.

Lane's and Gerald's collaborating to avoid conflict had resulted in the buildup of resentment in Lane that finally boiled over. Leaving the house when he was angry about Gerald's messiness may have prevented a blowout at the time, but it did not dispel the resentment caused by Gerald's inconsiderate behavior.

By keeping quiet about it to avoid conflict, Lane was actually reinforcing Gerald's messy behavior, giving him tacit permission to go right on doing the same thing. A better option for Lane would have been to address the issue with his partner when he first began to feel the frustration. It could have been done without built-up anger, and while it might have felt like conflict to these two conflict-avoidant people, it would have been without the force that stored resentment exhibits when it boomerangs.

THE RELATIONSHIP VERSUS

THE PEOPLE IN IT

"What a choice you've given me! Either I have to do something I really don't want to do, or I have to feel guilty because I've kept *you* from doing it."

My partner loves to be with a lot of people. She doesn't mind crowds. She is drawn to the excitement of high-visibility events. She is stimulated by the challenge of gaining access, getting there, fighting the mob, sharing an experience with thousands of strangers.

I don't like crowds, lines, any trouble with getting there or getting in. I like comfort, easy access, and seats on the aisle.

So she asked me if I wanted to go to this wildly anticipated Barbra Streisand concert in a stadium, saying that she had been offered two of the most expensive seats in the house as a *gift*. She was obviously eager to go. So what should I do now? Being a good partner means I should put my dislike of crowds aside and cheerfully endure the mob scene. After all, isn't the relationship more important than my personal intolerances?

If my lover were a friend who asked me to accompany her to this event, I would say, "No, thank you. I don't want to go," and that would be the end of it. My friend could go or not go to the concert. It would no longer have anything to do with me. But if my partner doesn't go because she prefers not attending without me, our relationship might be in crisis, or at least that's the way I was seeing it.

How does one arrange one's priorities in a situation like this? Am I obliged to do what she wants? Is she obliged to do what I want? Since she knows I don't like crowds, why would she be so persistent about my being in the middle of one? Since I know she loves to go where the action is, why would I not agree to indulge the person I care most about?

We've been at this for years; it is the inevitable consequence when two people who are very different from one another share a life. In such an instance the relationship does, in a sense, take on an existence of its own because it is the negotiating table of so many conflicting needs and interests. The problem is that too often we don't differentiate between the relationship and the people in it.

The obligation to be a good partner can cause you to ignore relating to your lover as a person, not as the arbiter of how well you are doing in your partnership role. Assumptions are made about the consequences "for the relationship" of decisions involving what both partners are going to do. The decisions appear to be dictated by the relationship, not by needs of the people in it.

You assume that if you don't cooperate, acquiesce, do what your partner wants to do she or he will feel deprived and/or angry. So, you do it, resent it, possibly even ruin it, only to learn later, perhaps, that you were wrong—it really wasn't all that important to the other person in the first place. Or you don't do what your partner wants to do, feel guilty, resent that, retaliate for being *so* compromised, and beat yourself up for being an inadequate partner.

Why didn't you learn earlier that it didn't matter that much? Because you were preoccupied with doing the right thing for the relationship, as if some power above were sitting in judgment of your performance as lover and companion.

I learned, for instance, that my assumption about my partner's being eager to go to the wildly anticipated concert was wrong. She wasn't really eager at all, just mildly interested. Too often we base our decision about the right thing to do on an assumption that may not even be correct.

Where do we get our ideas about what the "right thing" is to do in an intimate relationship? Is the right thing that which will keep you out of trouble, meet a lover's needs, ratify the legitimacy of this socially unsanctified partnership? Is it simply a matter of treating the person you love in the caring and supportive way you want to be treated yourself. Or is it all of the above?

Sometimes people believe that the right thing in a relationship is self-sacrifice. Giving up one's prerogatives and options *for the sake of the relationship* can make one feel like a victim, not a good position from which to lovingly reach out. When that happens, trust and goodwill between partners may become eroded, especially if one partner is doing something he or she really doesn't want to do. Negotiated compromise is much more conducive to the health of a relationship than one-sided self-sacrifice.

Ron and David

Ron and David came to me with the story of a long-term relationship they felt was coming to an end. They had been together ten years. For much of that time David had been the person "in charge" of the relationship—he made most of the decisions about how they would spend their time, money, and energy. That had been fine with Ron. He went along because he had no reason not to.

The relationship had worked until the last few months. Ron had begun opting out of David's plans. More and more he was inclined to make plans of his own, choosing to spend less of his time with David, who was puzzled about what was happening. When questioned, Ron said that he just needed some variety in his life, that he was tired of doing the same old things with the same old people. He wanted to explore his options a little more.

David did not take this development well. After several months of protesting to no avail, he told Ron that he really needed a full-time lover and that if this relationship didn't offer that he was ready to look elsewhere. David backed up his threat by immediately getting involved with a young man he met at the gym.

For a while Ron put up with David's dalliance, but when it seemed to be getting more serious he panicked. He didn't want to lose David, he had only wanted a little more independence. Now there was the possibility that he would have more independence than he had bargained for.

Ron decided it was time for some damage control. He made David a proposition—stop seeing the young man and they could resume their relationship as it had been in earlier times. Because it was Ron whom David really loved, he agreed.

It worked and it didn't work. Indeed, Ron stopped making plans of his own, but he found he could no longer just go along as he had before. He didn't *want* to do everything David planned. He'd had a taste of independence and he couldn't forget it. This was the dilemma as he saw it: be on his own without David or acquiesce to everything David planned—*do it for the relationship.*

Ron went to baseball games because David loved baseball. Ron was bored. He went to rock concerts because David liked that kind of music. Ron didn't. Ron left parties earlier than he wanted to because David didn't drink and was ready to go home when things got a little too raucous for him.

Ron did these things for the relationship, but he increasingly resented his loss of freedom. He felt victimized by his obligations to the relationship. Soon he became surly when he was with David, and the question of their future together was up in the air again.

Notably missing from Ron and David's partnership were good negotiating experiences. Earlier, when Ron took off on his own, there was no option for negotiation. Then, when Ron became wedded to the relationship rather than to David, there was no one there to negotiate with.

The first task was to help Ron separate the relationship from the people in it. It was David he had to deal with, David's differences from him, David's need to be in control, David's difficulty in understanding Ron's desire to have more independence. When Ron did things he didn't want to do "for the sake of the relationship," he was not dealing with David at all, and that is why it didn't work.

The second task was to help David and Ron learn to negotiate the conditions of their life together. There had to be participation by both in decision making, consideration of the interests of each person, an *integration* of plans that had previously suited only David or Ron. When they were able to negotiate a mix of activities that satisfied both, their relationship began to reflect who they were as people. The tail had stopped wagging the dog.

THE CHALLENGE TO GROW IN

RELATIONSHIPS—WHY IT IS

SO MUCH WORK

A main reason that relationships sometimes seem like so much *work* is that those skills so essential to dealing with intimacy are not taught anywhere. Of all the things we learn in school, how to be in an intimate partnership is missing in action. But, of course, we all need to know calculus, how to conjugate a verb, and what the capital of Belize is in order to live a good and fulfilling life. It is no wonder so many people are floundering in their efforts to have sound and enduring partnerships.

Feelings and relationships are two things that *every* human being must deal with, no matter who you are, where you are, or what your life is about. Yet there is no training for dealing with emotions or relationships in our institutions of learning.

Oh, yes, sometimes the practicalities of marriage are taught, but not the intricacies of intimacy—the expectations and the demands for closeness and openness, for selflessness. There is nothing in the curriculum about how to deal with the disillusionment that occurs when trust is betrayed, the skills that enable resolution, the courage to stick it out when frustration overwhelms reason.

The luckiest among us come from families in which these skills were taught, at least by example, but not many of us are that lucky. So we enter our gay and lesbian relationships as emotional novices, in a sense, learning as we go, carried along by goodwill and the determination to be successful in these liaisons that society says don't count.

And, yes, it does take work, sometimes painful work—probing and raw nerves and giving up defenses and redefining reality. It's scary stuff, but the payoff is in the process itself, the changing, growing, being alive, and inventing the future together.

CHAPTER 8

The Years Bring Change—
Coping with Transitions

"You're not the person I fell in love with. You've changed."

How many times I have heard this spoken critically, as though someone's changing was a violation of the I'll-never-be-any-different clause in the relationship contract. Over the long term everyone changes, but when partners set their psychological compasses according to where they perceive each other to be and one changes in any significant way, the other may see the change as betrayal.

INTERNAL CHANGES

One of the most difficult kinds of change to deal with is the change that comes from within the person—a shift in feelings, a reordering of values, a new plan for life ahead. If communication is good and everyone understands what is happening, such change can be accommodated with minimum stress. If there has been little or no talk about the shifts one partner is experiencing internally, and it is apparent that something different is happening, the situation is ripe for misinterpretation.

For instance, one partner becomes preoccupied with making a career change but hasn't yet decided to share these thoughts. The other partner knows something is up but is in the dark as to what. In the absence of information a vacuum is created. It isn't only nature that abhors a vacuum, most of us do. The in-the-dark partner begins to fill in the empty spaces, sometimes with disasters in the making.

"He's planning to leave me."
"The chemistry is over."
"She's involved with someone else."

Forcing discussion may not be your style, but in this instance your need to know is reason enough to lure your lover into telling you what is going on. Whatever is happening with one partner inevitably affects the other. By insisting on being let in on the process you may find out why your partner was reluctant to talk to you at this stage.

What you learn may not be what you want to hear, but it will give you an opportunity to make changes that can improve future communication in your relationship. Sometimes a person will hold back with a partner out of a fear of being laughed at, argued with, or pushed to make a certain decision prematurely. If any of those are reasons you are not being let in on your lover's internal deliberations you would want to know that, wouldn't you? How else could you make sure it doesn't happen again?

Maybe a change has occurred in your partner that neither one of you likes or understands. Let's say you are both willing to talk it over. Where do you start? One helpful approach is to try to trace the change back to a turning point. It might be a triggering event or an identifiable time period when something disturbing was going on. Perhaps the feelings about it went underground and need to be coaxed out.

Change does not occur isolated from experience and the reactions it provokes. Clarity emerges from retrieving emotions that have become hidden, putting them in the perspective of one's history, and exploring their relevance to what is going on currently.

EXTERNAL CHANGES

Internal changes are probably the hardest to ferret out and cope with, especially when the person has imposed a code of silence on himself or herself. Much easier to deal with are those changes that are external, out in the open, happening for all to see; changes involving such things as job status, career moves, or major shifts in income up or down.

CHANGE IN JOB STATUS

A job promotion could mean more responsibility and a greater investment of time away from home and lover. There may be conflict between the positive aspects of being successful and the negative consequences of problems engendered in the relationship. The matter of priorities reordered rises to the top of the list of concerns for the couple. This is a time to look carefully at the situation to see if there is anything to be negotiated. Don't foreclose on that possibility too soon.

Another potentially affecting issue may be feelings of envy on the part of the partner who was not promoted, especially if a lover's moving ahead creates a discrepancy in the prestige value of one's job versus the other's. Most of the people I know deny they feel competitive with their partners, but I don't believe it. I've been privy to the inner workings of enough clients to know that the competitive spirit is as alive and well in gay and lesbian relationships as it is in every other kind.

Because envy is not considered an admirable trait, the possibility is that it won't be expressed directly but might be acted on in some ambiguous way. Most of us have felt the discomfort of envy and wished we didn't have to feel that way, but burying the feeling to save face also buries the information your partner might need to help you work through these feelings.

I envy my partner's greater visibility in our community and the respect she is shown for her work wherever we go. If I denied that I have these feelings they would turn into resentment, which I would probably act out in some way that would create a whole new set of problems.

Instead I am free to say that I envy her and she then has the opportunity to tell me what a wonderful, important, and admired person *I* am. Get it out in the open. Envy may not be the classiest of emotions, but it is understandable and probably as universal as any of our flawed ways of reacting to life.

Rebecca and Peggy

I remember a client, Rebecca, who had been with her lover for fifteen years. When they first got together both were corporate employees functioning at about the same level. Peggy, who was younger, was described as a sweet, loving person, wonderful to be around. About five years into the relationship, Peggy was promoted to a supervisor's position, later to middle management, then to a vice presidency of her firm.

Rebecca, having advanced only to supervisor, tried hard not to be envious of her lover, but she had to admit that there were times when she felt jealous of Peggy's success. This was especially true on those occasions when she saw Peggy in action. Here was this strong, self-assured, assertive person, giving no quarter, besting her male counterparts, in charge and on top.

Rebecca looked wistful when she talked about this. She said she didn't like this Peggy—too cold and remote. She missed the sweet, loving Peggy she knew at home. As far as she was concerned they were two different people: good Peggy at home and bad Peggy at the office.

It took Rebecca a while to allow herself to admit to resentment and talk about it with Peggy. Airing this feeling made it less powerful, and eventually the resentment dissipated enough for Rebecca to integrate the two Peggys in her mind. She realized that she needed one, admired the other, and loved them both.

If the change your partner undergoes in job status is a downward move, he or she may be depressed and embarrassed. You want to be helpful, so your first move is to listen carefully to all of the feelings the person wants to ventilate. Forgo advice and problem solving until there has been sufficient opportunity for feelings to come out.

Second is the importance of maintaining the relationship as a safe haven and a source of affirmation. There are times when we must put our own agendas aside and be as available as possible to the person we share our lives with. If there is any place to look for comfort and support when outrageous fortune comes your way, it should be to this partnership, founded on the promise of love and support.

THE CLOSET

Certain changes involved in career moves may be particularly difficult for a gay or lesbian couple to integrate. For instance, one may be compelled to stay in or return to the closet in a new career. If one partner is out and the other must keep the relationship hidden, it devalues the partnership and could eventually erode the respect the openly gay person has for the one who is closeted.

I have heard stories that seem bizarre, though I know they are true, about the lengths some couples have gone to in order to conceal their relationship when they were convinced they had to do that to protect their careers. One client said she hid in the closet (appropriately) when her lover's coworkers appeared unexpectedly. Another told me that he introduced his long-time lover as a friend who had just dropped in for the evening when colleagues visited.

I sincerely hope that with the millennium such accommodation to bigotry will disappear. Relationships are hard enough without being dishonored from within. Is success in any career worth the indignity of living your life as a charade?

I hear some of you shouting "Yes, of course!" But I've seen enough people pull away from that position to know that it is not as popular or necessary as it used to be. And, of course, the more people do not hide the less imperative it will become to have to do so.

NEW PEOPLE

I have known situations in which the main problem one partner had with another's change in job status had to do with the threat of too many new people in their life.

"What effect will these people have on my lover?"
"How will this impact the relationship?"
"Will priorities change?"
"What will *I* have to do differently?"

We all fear the unknown to some degree. The question is, how do we handle it? Keep our fears to ourselves and just stew about such concerns? Or use the situation as an opportunity to reinforce honesty as a core element of our partnership? When I am willing to express my concerns to my partner, no matter how unflattering to me they are, I am ridding myself of the power that fear of the unknown can have over me.

INCOME SHIFTS

Like career moves, significant shifts in the income of one partner can be threatening to the other. Money has an enormous symbolic value in our society. It stands in for worth and signifies achievement. I find that many people are more secretive about their money than they are about anything else in their lives.

For example, clients will freely tell me their most guarded secrets—sexual fantasies they are embarrassed by, fears they are ashamed of, betrayals they regretfully confess to—but when discussing their money they become amazingly coy:

> "I make X amount of dollars now."
> "We paid X for our house."
> "The settlement I received was X."

I often wonder what they are thinking—that I will think more or less of them if I am privy to the amount of their income, the worth of their house, or the details of their assets? More likely, not talking about money is an ingrained habit learned in the family and supported by what passes for good manners in our society. How much or how little you have is imbued with meanings beyond the practical value of those dollars.

A shift in income involving a sudden influx of money to one partner can also be a threatening change. The other partner may wonder:

> "Will *I* have enough money to keep up?"
> "What if *I* can't afford to do the things my lover can do now? Will I be resented?"

This, of course, can only happen if the partners' finances are kept separate. If the threat of not being able to compete financially is privately held and not talked about, a feeling of inadequacy may ripen into anger, with the lesser-income partner paying for things she or he can't really afford and resenting it.

Hal and Robbie

For Hal and Robbie, life was pleasantly predictable until the day that something totally unexpected happened. Robbie got a phone call, and when he came away from the phone he looked as if he was in shock. Alarmed, Hal asked what had happened. Robbie reported that his Uncle Lewis had died—a heart attack, no warning, no illness, just keeled over and died. Robbie quickly learned that Uncle Lewis, a single man, had made Robbie the sole heir of a sizable estate. From that moment on, Hal's and Robbie's life was never the same.

There was the funeral, the gathering of relatives, and finally, the reading of the will. It took Robbie several days to realize that he was now a rich man. Much time was spent with the lawyer, going over Uncle Lewis's assets, the details of estate taxes, and the responsibilities that go with being heir to a person's complex holdings.

Once all this was over, Hal and Robbie settled into their familiar routines again. But there was a difference. Robbie now began to think like a person with money. If he saw something he liked in a store, he bought it, no second thoughts. He began talking about trips to places he and Hal could never have afforded before. The cautiousness that had marked their forays into dining out was now gone. They dined in the most expensive restaurants in the city.

Of course, Robbie picked up the tab on everything they did. No more figuring out who owed what, as they had always done. Hal was okay with this initially, but when Robbie began talking about a trip around the world, Hal started to feel anxious. *He* couldn't afford a trip like that. Robbie had been insistent on paying for their dinners out, but a trip around the world? Hal couldn't see Robbie laying out that kind of money for the two of them.

Hal was in a quandary. Robbie's enthusiasm for this trip seemed to grow with every new day. He just seemed to take it for granted that Hal would accompany him. Hal figured and refigured his finances. No matter how he stretched there wasn't enough money to make a significant contribution. Nevertheless, he found himself offering to undertake the expense of various legs of the trip. Robbie said that would be fine.

Hal wondered if Robbie had forgotten who he was. Robbie knew what Hal's income was. How could he agree to an outlay of money that he must know Hal didn't have? But now Hal was feeling adamant about not having his way paid. He was committing himself to expenditures right and left, until the day came when he began to panic. He was in over his head. He would have to go deeply into debt to make this trip. He didn't want to do that. He didn't know what to do, but he did know how he felt. He was furious with Robbie for creating this crisis.

Hal began to punish Robbie either by disagreeing with everything he said or by refusing to discuss the trip, saying he was tired of talking about it. Robbie was puzzled. He tried to find out what was wrong, but he got stonewalled by Hal. After weeks of this, Robbie began questioning if he wanted to be in a relationship with someone he couldn't even have a conversation with. Hal and Robbie were barely speaking to each other.

The breakthrough came one night when they went out to dinner and Robbie seemed to be spending a long time figuring out which credit card to use. Hal took this as a hint that *he* should pay for dinner. All of the anger he had built up against Robbie about money boiled over. Hal felt as if he couldn't help himself. He spewed out everything—his resentment at being placed in such a compromising position, his panic at having to spend money he didn't have, Robbie's insensitivity to the crisis he had created and to Hal's anguish about it.

When Hal finished, Robbie was astonished. He sat in silence for a few minutes. Then he reached over and took Hal's hand. He said he'd had no idea all this was going on, and, of course, he had been terribly insensitive. He said he saw now that he had been living in his own little world, dazzled by having this money and focused only on his own desires.

Hal felt greatly relieved to have the issue out in the open. Listening to Robbie, he realized how unfair he had been to him. The two partners were then able to talk about what had happened since the inheritance and how they would relate in the future to the matter of money. The silence was broken, and open communication was once more their bridge to each other.

An equally threatening change involves a downward shift in income. The threat to the other partner is usually about having to provide financial support that had not been necessary before. If there has been no previous negotiation about the sharing of expenses but an unspoken assumption that all would be shared equally, the need suddenly to be the primary provider can come as a shock.

Loss of any kind can take the wind out of your sails; loss of income can feel as if the boat is sinking under you. But what of the threat felt by the partner who now faces the prospect of supporting another adult, possibly for the first time? I find this is much more difficult for gay men to accept, especially if they operate on the notion that men should support themselves and not be supported (like a woman?).

It's really all a matter of programming and of deprogramming. If two people, any gender, love each other and are pledged to spend their lives together, what's the difference who pays for what? If the relationship is at the center of your existence, isn't that more important than accommodating to a social program organized around the heterosexual relationship model (where the man is *expected* to be the breadwinner)?

The "program" that says men should always support themselves did not have you and your lover in mind when it was written. Your plan for living should be organized solely around the needs of your unique partnership and what is happening in it at any given time. I mean, who's watching, anyway? Who's judging? Who's in charge here, *them* or you?

The best remedy for dealing with discrepancies in income is to do away with a let's-share-expenses-like-roommates formula and replace it with a let's-pool-our-money-like-permanent-partners one. Doing so is an act of faith in the future of the relationship. It is acknowledgment of the true sharing of a life. It is replacing fear of betrayal with the bond of trust. It is taking money out of the perspective of social symbolism and putting it in a relationship perspective, where it belongs.

THE IMPACT OF AIDS AND OTHER
SERIOUS ILLNESSES

I tell this story with some embarrassment. A long time ago (it seems like centuries) a male couple came to me to work on their relationship. One partner was in an advanced stage of AIDS. My office is in my home, and from the window I watched this couple arriving for their session. Sometimes the partner with AIDS would be so debilitated he would have to drag himself up the stairs. Watching them, I wondered why these two were putting so much energy into working on a relationship that, inevitably, would soon be over.

How chagrined I feel to have had such a thought! Now, years from that early experience, I understand what a profound need couples dealing with AIDS have to stay connected, to work through whatever obstacles to intimacy there may be. Love is precious right up to the last breath of life. It is the force that enables two people to grow closer even as they confront the prospect of moving apart.

So much in the relationship may have to be altered as a result of serious illness—future plans, the ways in which time and money are spent, the roles of the partners. As a consequence of this added stress, whatever relationship problems there may have been before can resurface with dramatic intensity. But the things that probably offer the biggest challenges to the couple's equilibrium are the changes in the psychological structure of the partnership.

We all have certain needs that shape how our relationships evolve. For instance, we need to feel safe—a loving partner is often idealized as having the *power* to keep us safe and comfortable. We need to feel worthwhile and wanted—a loving partner mirrors back to us an image of someone who is valued and desirable. And we need to have a sense of connectedness—a loving partner is there for us, a committed mate, a presence to rely on.

Critical illness threatens these structures. For instance, the partner who is sick may no longer feel like a powerful protector. If this person took care of many of the practical aspects of the relationship, the caregiving partner (I will assume for the moment that is you) may have to take on new responsibilities, losing in the process the comforting feeling that someone is there sharing the load, taking care of things.

Preoccupation with the practical and emotional demands of illness can make the ailing partner so self-absorbed that the mirroring function is short-circuited. Even though you know intellectually that this is a product of the illness, you may still grieve the loss of a lover's affirming behavior toward you.

For gay male couples, the inability of the partner with AIDS to feel sexual desire or to even have an erection can feel like a powerful loss. While this does not happen to all people with HIV, it can occur at different stages because of the progression of the illness, medications, depression, or drugs taken for depression.

One partner of a person with AIDS told me that because his lover was now sexually unresponsive to him, he couldn't help feeling unattractive. Their solution for this was twofold: His partner learned to approach sex intellectually rather than through intuition or sexual desire—though he might have no sex drive himself, when he saw his lover was aroused he knew what to do next. He might not feel desire, but he was *willing* to participate. Also, he made a special effort to convey to his well partner that he found him attractive, compliment him on his appearance, and convey his affection with loving looks.

Once again, talking about what is happening is crucial. How does either partner feel about the HIV-affected person's body? How afraid is the well partner of being infected? Is outside sex an acceptable alternative? In some situations I know of, the person with AIDS has often felt a burden lifted from him by knowing that his lover could go elsewhere for sex. In others, that idea was totally unacceptable, feeling like a devastating rejection.

There is no right answer. There is only what any two people decide is best for them.

Useful information on this topic is offered in Michael Shernoff's chapter in *Positively Gay*, titled: "Gay Male Sexuality: Exploring Intimacy in the Age of AIDS." Michael is a New York City psychotherapist who writes and does workshops on eroticizing safer sex.

One of the most difficult of all the trials of AIDS is that emotional connectedness may feel stretched thin as the illness competes for your partner's time and energy. While the commitment may be as strong as ever, the ability of the person with AIDS to be there for the other's needs is compromised.

For example, one person told me that a major loss in living with a partner's AIDS has been no longer being able to share activity around food. His lover had lost his appetite and all desire for food, not uncommon at some stages of the illness.

"Here's something we used to have fun with. Meals were a nurturing, bonding time, shopping, cooking, going out to eat. Now he often has no appetite. I cook, he tries, but he cannot eat. Meals are now a source of anxiety and stress and are a constant reminder of the illness."

If something like this is happening in your life, it is time to be creative. Alternative ways of mutual nurturing can be explored—what activities other than meals are of interest to both of you? How about snuggling up to watch video movies together, reading to each other, listening to music, discussing the state of the world, sharing the latest gossip, sitting quietly and holding hands?

What else can help? Understanding what is happening psychologically will keep reality in focus for both of you. Allowing others to pitch in and "take care of you"— whether that means doing the practical things, giving some TLC, or providing respite from caregiving—can help alleviate some of the everyday stress. These opportunities may be necessary only temporarily, or they may have to be integrated into the long-term picture.

If you are personally dealing with AIDS you might take advantage of the many support groups there are now in our community, some appropriate for you as a caregiver, some for your partner, and some for both of you together. No one needs to go through the AIDS experience alone at this point in time. There is help, understanding, information, and the chance to reach out to others, which in itself can be very therapeutic.

There is a certain predictability to the course of AIDS and to the emotions it produces. First there is the apprehension that comes with the diagnosis—fear of what's ahead, of what you will be faced with, of your ability to do what's expected of you. The partner with AIDS will probably undergo a change in self-image—less of a sense of being in control, more vulnerability, mood swings, and anger that seems to come from nowhere.

You may find *yourself* uncertain as to what it is okay to say or do. Is it all right to cry, to surrender to sadness, to allow anger, to give in to fear? The answer is that you will probably have no choice. It is natural to feel all of those emotions. It is inevitable that you will need to express them—somewhere, somehow.

I find that couples usually cope with HIV in much the same way they have coped with everything else in their relationship. Of course, there is more compassion, depth of feeling, and increased sensitivity to the needs of both partners. But in those moments when the illness and the demands of caregiving seem relentless, old coping mechanisms tend to emerge, including the ones that didn't work too well in the first place.

For instance, perhaps a struggle for control permeated your couple interaction before. The person who is

ill now has an acute need for attention and accommodation. Seeing this as the old bid for domination may trigger a desire to counter with a competing bid for control.
Hopefully, the impulse will be restrained.

Rather than slipping into the old pattern and *acting
it out*, you can *talk* about the feelings you are having. The
key is not to take what is happening personally. Easier
said than done, I know, but just as rejections of food and
sex are not rejections of you, neither are cries for attention efforts to control your life.

Sometimes, there is a belief that the expression of
any negative emotions may make the sick person sicker.
Negative feelings are unavoidably a part of any life-
threatening illness. The belief that only positive feelings
should be expressed between you and your partner is unrealistic. AIDS, or any illness that transforms your life,
produces feelings that may be startling in their intensity—anger, resentment, rage.

There is much to be angry about in relation to the
illness of AIDS.

"Why is this happening to us?"
"Why doesn't the government make more of an effort to
    find a cure?"
"Why are families so rejecting?"
"Why don't the doctors know more?"

You may be angry at your partner—he won't take his
medication when he's supposed to, he doesn't eat
enough, he is using too many painkillers, he's zonked
half the time and *really* unavailable. You feel impatient,
frustrated, furious with him.

The question is, what do you do with this anger? You
can vent it on innocent bystanders (not a good idea).
You can deny that it's happening (also not a good idea,

because it will come out in some other form). Or you can get your anger in perspective and give yourself permission to express it to your partner, who may need just such a wake-up call to stop rebelling against your efforts to be helpful.

Another way to deal with AIDS anger (and this goes for both partners) is to channel it into activism. Participate in an AIDS protest, write letters, lobby your government for more AIDS funding, get involved in AIDS education. Activism born of anger can transform frustration into productivity and self-affirmation.

There may be times when you absolutely have to get your anger out directly. Pound on your bed, scream at the wall, run through the street, scribble it all down. Your rage is righteous, correct, and natural. Just don't hurt yourself or anyone else in the process of ventilating it.

In any critical illness, both members of a couple should try to be as authentic as possible about their feelings. If you, as a caregiver, feel too weary to go on without a break, say so, make practical arrangements for one. This may produce a troubling ambivalence in your partner, who says "Go ahead, I want you to get away, you have to," but then lets it be known that he or she feels abandoned and furious when you decide to go.

Such ambivalence is understandable with someone who *feels* needy and vulnerable but is still functioning as a caring adult. Your partner should be allowed to express her or his feelings without canceling out a commonsense decision by you to take some time off.

Challenging the person who is ill to stretch emotionally can be very important. The challenge is to think of different (perhaps new) ways for the person to nurture, to be there, to show interest in the *caregiver's* life. It is about not giving in to the tyranny of the illness, but trying to be emotionally available enough to keep the connection strong.

With all the tribulations that HIV disease introduces, I see more couples using the time of the illness to achieve new depths of love and intimacy. This is much more likely to happen if feelings are openly shared. This is about being emotionally honest, not only with your lover but with yourself. No one expects you to be brave all the time. Give yourself permission to feel put upon, resentful, to want to flee. After all, it's what you *do*, not what you *feel*, that will count in the long run.

The impact on a relationship of AIDS, or any other life-threatening illness, is incalculable. It is indeed a test of the relationship bond and the ingenuity of the people involved. In the gay and lesbian community, we are now used to dealing with this crisis. We have books that tell us what to do, friends who tell us what *they* have done, social service agencies to deal with the practical and the psychological demands of living with AIDS.

With other serious illnesses, there is not this kind of community support—the caregiver information, the access to up-to-the-minute medical advances, peer group services such as "buddy programs," direct-action groups to push for a faster cure. Hopefully, some day the community at large will catch up, using the miracle of organized AIDS care programs as a model for how to deal with other catastrophic illnesses.

If compassion, dedication, and perseverance were all that was needed to cure AIDS, the gay and lesbian community would have banished the virus long ago. But that is not the case, so while research and treatment trials go on, we commit ourselves to working on those things we *are* able to do something about—such as learning how to integrate living with AIDS into a loving relationship.

I have chosen here to focus more on AIDS because it

is so pervasive in our community, but dealing with any critical illness that disrupts a couple's life can feel like fighting Goliath. Maybe there are ways in which different illnesses require different kinds of attention, but I believe that, in the main, the challenge is the same. It is about coping with the unexpected, being able to adapt to adverse reality, and internalizing the evidence that *you really are capable of dealing with it all.*

The challenge is to stay centered when the ground seems to be shifting under you. It's also about true grit— the courage to be there no matter what is happening, even in those moments when reality seems to slip away and you are sure you can't do what is expected of you, but you do it anyway. It's about love being tested and found to be more potent than you ever knew it could be.

EMERGENCE OF PROBLEMS
UNBARGAINED FOR

SPOUSAL ABUSE

It is difficult for most of us to understand spousal abuse. Why would someone batter the person he or she loves? How could anyone stay in a relationship in which there was such abuse? We usually associate domestic violence with heterosexual couples in which the man is the batterer and the woman is the victim. Is it abuse when two men are involved? Could there be a philosophically egalitarian lesbian relationship in which one partner batters the other? The answers are yes and yes.

Spousal abuse in the gay and lesbian community has been unacknowledged for a long time. In the early 1980s, the closet door first began to swing open on lesbian battering. Male domestic violence is just beginning to be acknowledged in the 1990s. Efforts to bring male-on-male battering to light often have been met with denial that it is anything more than just two guys going at it, as guys do.

The fact is that, as you read this, there are men and women in gay and lesbian relationships who are abusing their partners psychologically and physically, sometimes even to the point of putting their victims' lives in jeopardy. The movement to bring gay and lesbian spousal abuse to the attention of our community has been met in the past not only with denial that it was really happening but also with resistance to opening up a subject that might reinforce the negative stereotypes society already had about us.

For most readers, I assume, this topic will not be personally relevant. I include it here mainly for the sake of those whose relationships *are* complicated by abusive episodes that feel as if they are out of control. I include it also because, again, I think it's important for us to know what is going on in our own community.

To gain an understanding of what this is all about, I have made use of two among the excellent books on the subject: *Violent Betrayal: Partner Abuse in Lesbian Relationships* by Claire M. Renzetti and *Men Who Beat the Men Who Love Them* by David Island and Patrick Letellier.

What constitutes abuse? Putting together ideas from both of the books mentioned above, I offer the following overall definition: Domestic abuse involves a pattern of coercive behaviors—unwanted physical force, psychological and emotional abuse, material or property destruction—that one partner inflicts on the other in order to create fear in and exert control over that person.

The word *pattern* is essential to what we are dealing with here—repeated episodes of abuse over time. Not that a single episode early on isn't worth addressing, but it is the abuse that occurs when two lives are so enmeshed that escape feels impossible, or unthinkable, that we are mainly concerned with here.

The question most asked in any domestic violence situation is some version of "Why does the victim stay? Why not just go?" The reasons for people staying in abusive relationships are complex and include the following.

Remorse of the abuser, who *promises* to change.

Excusing destructive behavior because of diminished capacity (alcohol or drugs).

Compassion for a partner who experienced abuse as a child.

Abuser-forced isolation from family and friends, leaving only the abuser to go to for comfort.

Fear of retaliation if separation is attempted.

What one hears most often from victims is that they don't want the relationship to end, only the abuse.

So what do you do if you find yourself the victim in an abusive relationship? Much depends on the level of abuse. If it is only occasional and moderate, couple counseling can help, accompanied by individual or group therapy in which the abusing partner learns to accurately define his or her abusive behavior, control impulses, communicate *verbally* when angry, and take sole responsibility for abusive behavior—no blaming the victim.

If the abuse is severe and consistent, I suggest you seek professional counseling from someone who has expertise in the field of domestic violence. This is one way to assess the level of action you should be taking. If abuse persists and you feel powerless to control your own fate, it is time to ask for the help of advocates who can assist you with legal issues, safe places to be, and the process of healing your life. I suggest you read the books mentioned on page 211. They spell out the options available in the difficult business of removing yourself from an abusing situation.

Also, you can call the National Victim Center at 1-800-394-2255 (Monday through Friday, 8:00 A.M. to 5:30 P.M.). They provide information on where to go for help, and they are prepared to deal with same-sex abuse situations.

Domestic violence in the gay and lesbian community should no longer be treated as a nasty little secret or as something that someone just imagines is happening. Protecting the image of same-sex couples is not a reason to ignore the real danger that spousal abuse poses to the mental and physical health of members of our community. We should all be willing to open *this* closet door and face the reality of what we find inside.

SUBSTANCE ABUSE

Some years ago I was seeing a woman in therapy who was quite an impressive person. I'll call her Jeanine. She was a dignified woman who'd had a particularly successful professional career, from which she had just retired. She was articulate and insightful as she dealt with her late-in-life coming-out process. I'd seen her half a dozen times when one morning she came in and sat right down on the floor. Legs spread out, a silly smile on her face, she looked like a little kid preparing to play some child's game. I was startled at this change in behavior.

I asked Jeanine what she was doing and she said she had decided to be a little girl again, a bad little girl. She said she was tired of being responsible and following rules and she was just going to be bad. Then she pounded the floor with her fists and began to giggle uncontrollably. This behavior continued for the entire session. No matter what I tried she was unresponsive. She was with herself in the room, not with me.

The next time Jeanine came in she behaved just as erratically, and it was obvious that it was time for me to reassess her psychological state. It seemed inescapable that she had deteriorated mentally, but this transition had been very precipitous. Try as I might, I could not get anything out of her to help me understand what had happened. I was developing a plan to have her seen by a psychiatrist, and possibly be hospitalized, when I received a phone call from her lover. The conversation went like this.

> *"This is Mary Carter. You know who I am?"*
> *"Yes, I know you are Jeanine's lover."*
> *"I want to tell you something that I think you should know."*
> *"Go ahead."*
> *(Ordinarily I would have been much more circumspect with such a call, but I was worried enough about Jeanine to let Mary talk to me.)*
> *"You know Jeanine has been acting different lately?"*
> *"Yes."*
> *"What I think you don't know is that she now starts every day by drinking half a pint of vodka with breakfast. She drinks more through the day and is usually shitface by evening. She didn't do this before. I mean, she's been a steady drinker for twenty years, but now that she's retired the constraints are gone. It's gotten much worse. I don't know what to do."*

I was astonished. It had never occurred to me that Jeanine was *drunk* in my office. Psychotherapists can, and often enough do, miss picking up on alcoholism unless the person comes in with that as the presenting problem or talks about problem drinking directly. I was chagrined that I, too, had missed the clues.

I asked Mary if she would come in with Jeanine and say what she had just told me in front of her. She said she would, and she did. That was the beginning of Jeanine's recovery, involving thirty days in an in-patient alcoholism treatment facility followed by regular AA meetings, indefinitely after that.

Mary was able to help her partner because she *saw* what was happening and took action. It isn't always that simple. You may not witness the abuse occurring as Mary did, and many partners ignore signs of alcoholism or drug abuse even if they do see it because they do not want to believe it is happening. The person abusing is not the only one who practices denial.

It is well documented that alcohol and drug abuse have been a problem in the gay and lesbian community. It is easy to understand why. For many years the primary social outlets for gay people were the bars. Negotiating a positive gay or lesbian identity in a homophobic society can be an uphill battle.

Many of us have *internalized* society's antigay bigotry and struggle from within to feel okay as people. We have endured the ignorance and prejudice of bigots and just plain unenlightened folks, some of whom even love us as individuals. All of this hurts. Alcohol and drugs have historically been palliatives for the stress of these experiences.

Now there are alternatives to the bars as places to gather, such as gay-oriented cultural and political events, religious houses of worship, community centers, athletic games, and special-interest groups. It is easier to develop a positive gay or lesbian identity. Also it is no longer socially acceptable to express blatant antigay bigotry, at least in most places. Is there less reason to drink or use drugs *because* you are a gay man or a lesbian? Yes. Are people still doing it anyway? Some are, some always will, but there are differences.

Young people are not developing the "habit" of alcoholism, as many older gays and lesbians did in the oppressive years before the Stonewall riots launched the new gay rights movement. But, while gay men are more health conscious generally than they were before, there appears to be a growing tendency among some in the younger gay male community to dance away their AIDS worries under the influence of powerful designer drugs.

Since these drugs are being used in a "recreational setting," the prevailing rationale is that this is casual use, but many of these mind-altering substances are addicting and coming off them usually takes a heavy toll on the body. They are anything but health enhancing.

When does any of this constitute "abuse"? Traditionally, the answer from the substance abuse treatment field has been when drinking or drug use interferes with the ability to function in your career or job, primary partnership, relationships with family and friends, and any other important areas of your life. How do you know when you, or a partner, is abusing? That's a tough one because part and parcel with substance abuse comes the tendency to *deny* that it is happening.

Also, substance abusers can be astute about hiding their drinking or drug use. If, for instance, you are concerned about the possibility that your partner might be abusing, you may confront and get brushed off. Then what? One approach many have found helpful is to go to Al-Anon and let it be known that you are doing so. The message is: "You may not want to deal with this problem but *I'm going to.*"

If you think your partner has developed a drinking problem, or if you are concerned about your own drinking, it is important not to ignore what AA calls that elephant standing in the middle of your living room. There is a great deal of help out there now. Alcoholics Anonymous has meetings everywhere in the world. In most cities they now have gay or lesbian meetings. It is easy to connect with AA. Just look in the white pages of the phone book for the AA office in or near your city. Call and they will send you a directory that will have meetings marked for all kinds of features, including "gay" (G) or "lesbian" (L).

Al-Anon is for anyone who is involved with a person who is abusing alcohol. If the problem is with drugs, any gay and lesbian center should be able to direct you to a gay-oriented Narcotics Anonymous (NA) or other twelve-step program in your area. NA is also listed in the phone book.

Be alert to signs of excessive use. Don't enter into a conspiracy of silence if you think a serious problem is developing. Talk to your partner about his or her drinking or drug use. Talk about your own use, if that is what concerns you. Get it out in the open.

Confronting the problem may be especially hard to do if what is happening is that *both* of you are slipping into problem drinking or drug use. Reinforcing each other by not dealing with the problem is easily interpreted as permission to abuse. Breaking into this pattern can be the move that rescues one or both of you from a downhill slide that is hard to stop without help.

People who become dependent on alcohol or drugs often come to rely on the substance they are using as if it were their only friend. Their real-life partners take a backseat to the cycle of craving, satisfying that craving, recovering, and craving again. The cycle is a compelling force to compete with.

Alcohol or drug use "triangulates" an intimate partnership. It is no longer about just the two of you. Now, it's you, your partner, and the substance. The competing demands of this third presence can sabotage the love and affection that were there before. If this is happening in your relationship, don't stick your head in the sand. Don't let alcohol or drugs hold you hostage. Take action. Get help.

RENEGOTIATING THE "CONTRACTS"

Look beneath the surface of any partnership and you will discover the intersecting "contracts," mostly unspoken, that give form and direction to the relationship. How these contracts evolve is a function of what the partners need from one another. Perhaps you are a person who doesn't like making any more decisions than you have to. You need your partner to take on that responsibility whenever possible, and that is what happens. This contract didn't require negotiation, it just evolved, and it became one of the contours of your life together.

But what happens when there is a change—in you, or in your partner? How do you renegotiate an agreement that was never negotiated in the first place? This can be difficult, because while there may *be* a shared reality there may not be shared perception of what that reality is. For instance, for years you have been doing certain chores around the house. That was okay for a long time, but now you have some new projects in your life and you don't want to continue using your time that way. You tell your partner that you want to change the arrangement.

Your partner says, "What arrangement? We never had an arrangement."

You say, "I did those things because you didn't want to."

Your partner answers, "That's not true. I would have been glad to take on those chores, but you were already doing them."

The fact is, your beloved never offered to relieve you of the responsibilities in question. There didn't seem to be any reason to. The "arrangement" *was* that you were the one who would take care of those particular chores. Unspoken contracts are usually based on unchecked-out assumptions.

Because the years do bring change, identifying the contracts of your relationship, and checking to see if changes are in order, can help to keep what goes on between the two of you satisfying and relevant. As a way of doing this, think about the various aspects of your life together.

Who does what on a regular basis?
Is that arrangement still okay?
Do you know how that arrangement came about?
If it's not okay, what changes do either of you want?
What changes are either of you *willing* to make?

Doing this on a regular basis is a strategy for coping with the inevitable transitions that life brings to any relationship.

One recurring theme that I see grows out of the notion of an *unspoken contract* made at the beginning of the relationship that neither partner will ever change. That is absurd, of course, but not so to the person who doesn't want to be reminded of the unwanted passage of years, or that the image of the person he or she fell in love with has to be readjusted.

I was distressed one day when my lover came home

shorn of her beautiful long hair. She said the haircutter had misunderstood when she said to take off a little more than usual. While her haircut was stylish and becoming, I hated it. I had to ask myself why I was having such a strong reaction, because she looked just fine. I didn't want to admit the truth, which was that her long hair made her look like the twenty-nine-year-old I was attracted to twenty-one years before. I felt betrayed, as though I had been robbed of the image that made *me* feel twenty-one years younger.

Such irrational, but understandable, reactions to change demonstrate how important it is to deal as openly as possible with the feelings generated by it. Keeping the negotiating process alive and working assures that you will be dealing realistically with whatever transitions there are.

CHAPTER 9

The Outside World—An Ongoing Force in Your Relationship

The quality of any intimate relationship is influenced by two kinds of forces: internal (how the partners treat one another); and external (how other people, events, and the tenor of the times affect a couple's life). Rarely does any relationship exist in isolation. One usually *has* to deal with a myriad of influences, expectations, and people who can impact your partnership positively or negatively.

What is going on in your country, city, subculture, family, and friendship network is going to have a significant effect on what goes on in your intimate relationship. Like it or not, you cannot hide from the world; it comes to your door, invades your thoughts, shapes your opinions, and colors your life. Sometimes this outside world is an energizing force, sometimes an inhibiting one. Let's start with the good part—energizing forces.

EXTENDED GAY AND LESBIAN FAMILY

AS A SUPPORT SYSTEM

As a young person, I expected that my life would be that of a Gypsy. Not rooted in family or community, I thought I would wander from one scene to the next, forming new relationships with little continuity and no ties. I did live like that for a while, peripatetic and unattached. I knew a lot of people. When I thought it was time to move on I did, and then I knew a lot of other people.

The real problem was that I felt different. I didn't seem to fit into any social scene. I was an outsider without an understanding of what that actually meant. It was as if I had the wrong script. It never worked. I just accepted that this would be my life, being on the periphery of one group or another.

How wrong I was. Slowly entering the gay world in midlife, I came to understand it all. I finally belonged somewhere, fit in, made attachments, developed a family of my own. What a difference this acceptance of myself, this personal redefinition, becoming open and activist, has made for me. I can't imagine life without the chosen gay and lesbian family I now have.

I look around me and I see generations of friends, some people who were in their twenties when I first met them twenty or more years ago, who are now middle-aged themselves, gray in their hair, coats and ties and dress-for-success pantsuits replacing the activist garb of the 1970s gay liberation movement. We assemble now for community events and benefits, not rallies in the street, though the opportunity to get out there to protest yet another egregious governmental act is still welcomed. The activist ethic is there; it just plays out differently.

Whatever the nature of your gay or lesbian life, the importance of having a chosen gay family cannot be overemphasized. I hear stories of people whose biological families refused to attend their commitment ceremonies. "I just filled *my* section with our friends," one woman told me. Our gay and lesbian friends fill in for us not just the empty seats but those places in the heart that are left bereft when our biological families opt out of our lives—or choose to limit contact.

I am repeatedly reminded of how persevering and strong the bond of a chosen gay family can be. Many years ago, once again in the 1970s, I conducted a therapy group for gay men and lesbians that went on for seven years. I recently learned that members of the group have stayed in touch, one gay man regarding an older lesbian in the group as his big sister, spending holidays with her, bringing his boyfriends to meet her, traveling to her bedside as her own life was ending.

A client told me that he belonged to a friendship group that had formed as a result of AIDS, ten young men who spend time together regularly, not drinking and bar-hopping but socializing, playing bridge, watching movies, providing a bulwark against loneliness or the need to search for sex on the street. They have been doing this together for over a decade. They bring new lovers into the group, but always the core "family" is there to be depended upon.

My dear friend Paul Monette often started our dinners together by asking, "Well, what's the family gossip?" When Paul heard that a close friend of mine had died suddenly and unexpectedly, he offered, "Now remember, I'm here if you need emotional support about Stan." Paul was weeks away from his own death at the time, but concern for his gay family was always at the forefront of his mind.

At Paul's memorial service, the actress Judith Light, in her eulogy, said tearfully that Paul was the brother she had never had. For me Paul was the brother (a very special one) I did have, along with other sisters and brothers who make up my gay family. These are the people with whom we spend holidays, celebrate birthdays and anniversaries, and share the joys and tribulations of our lives.

It isn't a perfect family. There are instances of anger and resentment, jealousy, hurt feelings, and periods of not speaking. But isn't that like many families you know? I say, "I don't want to see so-and-so anymore because I don't like the way he behaved." My partner chides me, calls for a little more flexibility and adaptability, reminds me that the price you pay for keeping your friends over the years is putting up with their flaws. She's right, of course. I relent.

I emphasize the importance of extended gay and lesbian family because I believe that those ties, that connection, can contribute greatly to the strength and stability of any ongoing gay or lesbian relationship. Isn't that, after all, what we are aiming for in our own partnerships—connectedness, the tie that affirms, and the bond of friendship.

I am troubled when I hear that a gay or lesbian couple has few or no gay friends. While nongay friends may be sincerely supportive of your relationship, it is support absent the deeply felt, shared sense of identity that other gay people can bring to their friendship with you. It is gays who know the subjective experience of being different, the dilemmas of coming out, and the struggle to find, build, and maintain a same-sex partnership.

While we may indeed want variety in our social contacts, there is something indefinably affirming about knowing that those around us understand essentially what we are because it is what they are, too. The same is true for our relationships' being validated through interaction with others whose lives have the same contours as ours. If you do not already have a circle of gay friends, a chosen family, I heartily encourage efforts to seek out this gift of kinship for yourself.

INVOLVEMENT IN THE ORGANIZED
GAY AND LESBIAN COMMUNITY

"I'm not a joiner!"

How often I have heard this as I've tried to convince a gay or lesbian couple to become involved in the organized gay and lesbian community. Is this resistance to giving up one's identity to a group—"I don't want to lose my individuality"—or is it internalized homophobia, shyness, or just plain inertia? After all, I am not talking about hooking up with the Elks, the Shriners, or the Eastern Star. I am talking about participation in *our* community—something personally relevant that I believe can enhance the mental health of any gay or lesbian person.

Just as a chosen gay family can be energizing and supportive, so the organized gay and lesbian community can offer comfort and affirmation. It is where people labor to actualize the dream—eliminating the stigma of being gay, changing the world's attitudes toward us, and providing safe places for gays to assemble, learn, help, enjoy, and build relationships.

Being part of the organized community highlights the linkage to gay and lesbian people of the past and the future. You become more than a bystander to history.

You can be part of the unfolding story of a constituency inventing itself, a movement unifying its disparate elements into a community. And, important for our purposes, involvement in this community is an antidote to the sense of being an outsider that many of us have grown up with.

Society attempts to keep our relationships outside the boundaries of acceptance, refuses to sanction our unions or recognize that our partnerships are family. That is why we need community to reflect the reality of our lives and give our committed partnerships the recognition they deserve.

Perhaps community involvement is already a force in your couple life. You know a little, or a lot, about what's available for you. If that is not true, you should know that there are gay-oriented opportunities for almost anything you want to do as a couple. If you are into sports there are tennis and softball leagues that hold tournaments all over the country, ditto swim meets and skiing and running events, and, of course, there are the gay games, now a major tradition of our community.

There are choruses and bands, film festivals, gay theater and gay bookstores, religious groups of all persuasions, gay and lesbian community centers, hot lines to work on, computer bulletin boards to make contact through, and a great variety of organizations that assist gay youth, seniors, minorities, or any gay or lesbian person in need of help.

Political organizations need volunteers, social and educational groups offer ways to make contact, learn, and share lives. Male and female couples meet in many cities to have potlucks and go on trips. And fund-raising events are ever present opportunities to mix and do good for the community.

I've only scratched the surface of the kinds of activities available to gay and lesbian individuals and couples in our world. These are nonalcohol- and nonsex-related situations providing outlets for socializing and constructive involvement with other gay people. It isn't a perfect gay world, but it's ours and it has much to offer if you can give it your energy and open your life to it.

NONINTERGENERATIONAL GAY AND LESBIAN LIFE—NO MODELS TO GO BY

If there is one word to describe what most gay and lesbian people primarily hope for in their relationships it would be *continuity.* Too many of us subscribe to the myth that we are neither capable nor inclined to achieve long-term happiness in same-sex partnerships.

That is a myth, because there are quite enough long-term couples around to debunk the notion that gay and lesbian relationships *can't* have a long life. The problem is that there is so little cross-generational socializing in the gay community that the real-life evidence of longevity isn't easily visible and accessible.

In the heterosexual world, intergenerational contact is readily available in families. Plenty of moms and pops, aunts and uncles, and grandmas and grandpas have been together long enough to demonstrate that long-term relationships are possible and likely.

It is the ethic of heterosexual marriage that people stay together. Even though this does not work out much of the time, this is still the ethic that shapes expectations. Nobody officially gets married for five years, or until passion wanes or looks fade. They *expect* permanence, and that expectation is constantly reinforced by many of the entities that support marriage: family of origin, religious teaching, workplace benefit programs, and the body of laws governing entitlements. For gays and lesbians, what is too often misguidedly reinforced is the tradition of failure in same-sex relationships.

"Are John and Tom still together?" "Are you still with Mary?"

Another reason for the myth of impermanence is the invisibility of older, long-term couples in the gay world. Gays and lesbians tend to socialize fairly exclusively in their own age groups. The twentysomethings and thirtysomethings do not much associate with the older gays, who are more likely to be in long-term relationships. The ethic, therefore, is that gay relationships are like a revolving door, you're in there for a while and then you're out, then in again with someone else. That's what you see around you. That's what you expect.

The revolving door ethic seems to be especially prevalent among young lesbians. I was shocked recently when I gave a talk to a lesbian professional women's group. Those present were in their twenties, thirties, some early forties. They agreed with one another that being in a lesbian relationship was perilous because other lesbians were always out to steal your partner.

"It's best not to go out too much if you want to keep your relationship," one volunteered.

Heads nodded around the room. This was apparently a shared belief. For a moment I thought I was back in the fifties, when lesbian life was conducted in tight little friendship circles with relationships so intertwined that friends became lovers and friends again until everyone was an ex-lover of everyone else. There were no social outlets for lesbians outside the friendship circle, which consequently took on a hothouse quality emotionally.

But now we live in the big wide wonderful world of an open community where people don't have to hide and there are many places to meet other women. What was going on?

I asked this group if they knew many long-term lesbian couples. No, they didn't, nor did they know where to find them. It was as if such an entity might not even exist, so of course they believed that it would not come to pass for them, though they all insisted that a committed partnership for life was what they wanted.

I can't help but think that the revolving door ethic is part of the problem. Relationships take work. It is easier, perhaps, to blame a breakup on the predatory lesbian community than it is to take an honest look at what is going on *in* the relationship. If you can tell yourself that this is just the way it is with lesbians, you may be able to justify abandoning a relationship rather than attending to what might be wrong with it—easier, quicker, and the expectation of impermanence is reinforced.

So, I challenged those young women to do two things: Make a special effort to find some older lesbians who have been in a partnership for a long time, and stop reinforcing the revolving door ethic by talking about it and supporting one another in believing it.

Whatever social structures exist in the gay and lesbian community today are there because somebody took the trouble to create them. Yes, there is a lack of opportunities for intergenerational socializing. Yes, this does have a negative effect on young people who are trying to maintain permanent partnerships without role models, so somebody out there needs to think through what can change that. Somebody needs to create a meeting ground for younger and older, a vehicle for intergenerational socializing. Maybe that somebody is you.

OTHER PEOPLE'S RELATIONSHIPS

What do you do when your friends who have been in long-term relationships *do* break up? It is especially painful if it wasn't expected, and can often raise questions such as "Could this happen to me?" and "Will *my* lover leave *me* someday for someone else?" Whatever insecurities you might have regarding your relationship may float right up to the surface. So, what do you do about it?

You may need to reassure yourself by talking openly with your partner about your feelings. It is not unusual to fear that breakups can be contagious, but people do not break up because someone else does it and it looks like something interesting to do. They break up because there are problems in their relationship they have not dealt with. So, the real question is, are there problems in *your* relationship that aren't being dealt with? A friend's breakup may act as a wake-up call in that regard.

At the other end of the continuum is the couple whose relationship is longer-term than most of those around them, who have become the "model couple." Such longevity is to be celebrated, but sometimes the celebration has its oppressive side. If yours is the "model couple" story, you know that the downside is that others will want your life as a couple to be exemplary at all times.

You're not supposed to have unresolved conflicts or be anything but kind and loving to one another. You *are* supposed to present a solid front of happiness no matter how you happen to be feeling and never let it be known that there is trouble in paradise. You wouldn't want to disappoint all those people who are depending on you to be the exception to the "rule" that gay and lesbian relationships don't work, would you?

Being a model couple because you have weathered a

significant number of years together is great, but you shouldn't let your friends' need to deny reality ever be a force in your relationship. Every couple has problems at one time or another, and you should have the luxury of sharing your "bad patches" with others, if you choose to do that. Conflict goes with the territory of living together. Having to cover up conflict *in order to maintain an image* of being a model couple can be inhibiting and isolating. Don't let that happen to you.

FAMILIES: THE ONES YOU DIDN'T CHOOSE

My mother's funeral was cryptside, chairs on the grass, a sunny bright Southern California day. Relatives on *both* sides of my family (maternal and paternal) came from around the country, which was surprising to me since my parents had been divorced for forty-five years. My father was there with his fifth wife.

I opened and closed the ceremony, my sister and niece spoke, a cousin sang, and Terry told a story about how my mother had once admonished a tour bus driver in Las Vegas for making an antigay remark. Everything that involved "immediate family" included Terry—she wore the black mourner's ribbon and was described by the rabbi as a member of Mother Eva's family.

That seems about as integrated as you can get, unless you consider that we were sitting in front of two of the crypts that would be Terry's and mine, alongside Mom and Dad for all eternity. How's that for family integration?

This is a good story. The family stories of gay and lesbian couples are not always like this. This is the other long-term relationship, not the one with your partner but the one with your partner's parents and relatives. It's the one you didn't sign up for, but it comes as part of the package.

Your family is either making it all more wonderful by embracing your spouse or is making it all more difficult by rejecting or ignoring the most important relationship in your life. In any case, they are there—these families—for better or for worse, an inevitable outside force in your partnership. The question is, how strong is the force and how much control do you have over its effects?

In *Permanent Partners* I described the different kinds of familial relationships gay and lesbian couples tend to have, depending on how much the family is let in on the truth and what prejudices they do or don't bring to the situation. The first three categories occur when disclosure has been made to the family.

The *All-Embracing Family* is self-explanatory. Everything is out in the open, and a lover is integrated into the family in the same way a heterosexual spouse might be. Sometimes it works out even better with gay male couples, where a mother who might feel competitive with a daughter-in-law as the other woman in her son's life has no such feelings about her son's lover.

The All-Embracing Family talks about gay issues as if they were normal subjects for discussion, which they are. Gay and lesbian relationships are given the respect they deserve, and family members even become advocates in the fight against antigay discrimination.

These are the parents who often belong to Parents and Friends of Lesbians and Gays (P-FLAG), helping others understand and accept their gay and lesbian family members. Such support goes a long way toward validating the same-sex partnerships that our society tends to invalidate. In the All-Embracing Family, support for the gay or lesbian couple is public and unconditional.

Then there is the *Arm's-Length Family.* Being gay is

known about, but it never gets dealt with. If you are in this kind of situation, you avoid the topic of gayness as much as your family does. You are a coconspirator, reinforcing for them and possibly for yourself that being gay or lesbian should not be discussed because it is an unpleasant subject nobody wants to hear about.

Unpleasant subject? The central organizing fact of your life is an unpleasant subject? Your ability to love another person, your desire to create a family with that person—these are unpleasant subjects? Avoidance of discussion about being gay is avoidance of your most authentic self. You are offering a fraction of your being for anyone to experience when you become part of the conspiracy of silence about being gay.

Agreeing with your family's admonition not to tell anyone else forecloses on the possibility of understanding and acceptance that might be forthcoming from other relatives or friends of the family. I have found that grandmothers are particularly surprising when it comes to accepting gay or lesbian family members. Perhaps it is the wisdom of age, or maybe grandmothers are not as invested in the reflection on them that parents often worry about.

Why do people cooperate with a dehumanizing "don't tell" agenda? Usually it is out of fear of being cast out by the family. For years I have been reminding people that they are adults now who may love their families but do not *need* them in the same way they did as children, for survival. Here's my standard statement: "Your parents need you much more than you need them now, therefore *you* should make the rules for how you are going to relate to one another."

If you are in an Arm's-Length Family like this, I hope you will consider taking charge of the situation, invoking reality, and giving the folks a chance to know you as the whole person you are.

The *Pretend-You-Don't-Exist Family* is the worst-case scenario. It does happen, though with all the enlightenment about being gay and lesbian that is around today I see such rejection occurring much less than ever before. Nevertheless, if it happens to you it can feel devastating to have disclosed to people who have played such a critical role in your life and then been rejected for it.

So you *have* told your family, and they are unable to get past their prejudices to deal rationally with you. They are choosing to deprive themselves of your presence in their lives rather than pushing past ignorance to allow new information to illuminate old beliefs. Bigotry forecloses on growth, demands a closed system.

Once you have tried it all to no avail—talking, bringing them books to read, pleading, arguing, showing them your sadness and your anger—it is time to let go, to deal with the loss. The most important thing is not to internalize the prejudices that have immobilized your family. This is about them, not about you. It is defeating, frustrating, maddening, but it is something you can recover from once you have gone through the inevitable grieving.

Your life is about your own loving relationship, a place to go for comfort, just as "home" is where *you* live, not where your family lives. What has been abandoned is not you but a mythical child who is best left behind. You are not the product of someone else's stifling fantasy. You are your own creation, real, self-sustaining, and free.

The next two categories occur when the family has not been disclosed to. The *Totally-in-the-Dark Family* doesn't really know you are gay. You haven't given them any clues, and they haven't figured it out. One unfortunate product of this is that they have no reason to treat your lover as anything but a friend—separate beds when you visit them, no touching, no kissing, no affectionate glances.

You sanitize your living quarters when the family visits you. Censor. Monitor. Pretend. Exhausting. Is it really worth it? But you can't really blame the folks if you haven't given them a chance to understand. Are you sure this barrier between you is absolutely necessary?

This is a question to ask also if you are in a *We-Suspect-But-We-Don't-Really-Want-to-Know Family*. They know, you know they know, they know you know they know, but a grand silence surrounds the entire subject. You don't discuss anything that might trigger the verboten topic. You discuss *them* and *their* lives.

In this form of the charade, your lover is demoted to your "roommate." If there is a slip into even an affectionate glance, the family looks the other way. You are embarrassed to show your feelings for your partner. The truth is being held hostage here. Is this any way to run a loving relationship? Everyone involved deserves a reassessment of their ability to handle the truth.

If yours is an All-Embracing Family, you have probably earned that blessing. If not, I hope you will rethink what you want from a relationship with your unchosen family. Change is always possible, but it must begin with you. Question your fears. Take the risk. The outcome can be more freeing than you would ever expect.

ROLE REVERSAL: THE NEED TO

PARENT A PARENT

The first sign of trouble with my father came when he asked us to come over one day because he was "having a little trouble" with his checkbook. When we saw what the "trouble" was, we were stunned. This was a man who had made millions of dollars in complex real estate deals. Now suddenly it appeared that he couldn't complete the writing of a single check.

His checkbook stubs were scribbles, no way to know the amounts or the payees of any checks. Then he brought out a stack of bills, all months behind, a jumble of credit card statements, bills from his house accounts at restaurants, and alarming dispatches from the Internal Revenue Service.

When we added it all up, it was a staggering amount of money he owed, partly because he'd been unable to figure out how to pay the bills and partly because the money, brilliantly earned but poorly managed, was simply *gone*. We took over his finances, which meant contacting creditors to advise that he was beyond being able to pay these bills. Some were amazingly understanding, and some were monstrous. (Eventually, and it took several years, the creditors all went away.)

Next was his car. His driver's license had expired. He had unpaid traffic tickets and was in litigation over two accidents he'd caused. We confiscated the car. This was a big step to take, because in Los Angeles having a car amounts to having control of your life.

Since he had only his Social Security as income, we had to supplement it so he would have a place to live. We were already paying for my mother's nursing home, and the expense of having two aging and dependent parents started to feel overwhelming.

I asked myself, "Why didn't I see this coming?" The fact is, I had never given a thought to the possibility of having to support either of my parents. Is this an artifact of being gay? Since most of us don't have children, do we not focus sufficiently on planning for the future? How shortsighted we can be.

The fastest growing segment of the American population is the group over eighty-five; next fastest is those over seventy-five. That means that your parents, if they are still alive, may well survive to an age when they will require your help because they are physically or mentally debilitated or in need of financial assistance. It's surprising how many of us feel blindsided to find ourselves suddenly in a role reversal, parenting a parent. It's something most people don't want to think about, much less plan for.*

The kind of assistance needed by an aging parent can vary from emotional support for one who is widowed and lonely to full responsibility for the physical and mental well-being of a frail or mentally incompetent mother or father. It is not only the loss of a functioning parent that is disorienting but the challenge to do something you've never done before, something hard, possibly unpleasant, a stretch for the mind and emotions.

Of course, many factors enter here. What kind of a person was this parent to begin with? What has the quality of the relationship been so far? What other siblings are there to help? What resources are available? What is going on in your own life? If you happen to adore a parent who has been nurturing and loving, it is a pleasure to return the favor and become a loving caretaker.

If the relationship has been rocky, it is more difficult to make whatever sacrifices are necessary—more

*Whether your planning for a parent might involve in-home assistance or placement in a residential facility, help abounds. A referral directory listing various services is available from the National Association of Professional Geriatric Care Managers, 1604 North Country Club Road, Tucson, Arizona (602) 881-8008. An excellent book to consult is *Parentcare: A Commonsense Guide for Grown-up Children* by Lissy Jarvik and Gary Small.

difficult, but no less an obligation. Being in a long-term relationship does carry with it the possibility that there will be aging parents on one or both sides. But, whomever these parents belong to, it is both partners who are bound to be affected.

There may have to be compromises, financial and personal, with money and energy diverted to the care of a parent. There will be heightened feelings, resentment perhaps, jealousy regarding time spent away from the relationship, interference with plans. All of these are par for the course unless the partners are absolutely in sync about how money should be spent, the compelling nature of the parental bond, and how necessary it is to meet this obligation. Even then, feelings may at times brim over.

I am fortunate. I have a partner with whom I am in sync about all these things. Her equilibrium balances out my anger—the rational part about my father's not providing for his old age, the irrational part about my parents growing old and dependent. The burden is especially mine because her parents are deceased and, for reasons too byzantine to go into here, were never in our lives at all. Mine were always an integral part of our partnership.

For many people this issue of role reversal is the most emotionally disturbing part of parenting a parent. This is the person who is supposed to take care of you. Now you have to become the authority figure. You have to make the decisions and carry them out even if it means being firm and giving orders.

Dealing with the feelings that go along with this often unplanned-for development in your life is usually key to how well you are going to cope. If it is *your* parent who needs the caretaking, you may well feel guilty about the financial burden as it affects your partner, especially at those times when he or she is grumbling about it.

If there are grumbles from your partner, don't try to cut them off; grumbling is a natural outlet. Probably you won't want to hear it, because you don't want to feel that surge of guilt. Well, you didn't *want* this to happen, you didn't *make* it happen, and you *can't* make it go away— but you *can* keep the lines of communication open for some healthy complaining.

Putting up with the guilt without cutting off your partner sends the message "I can't help that this is happening but I care how you feel about it."

Of course, it would be better if you could dispense with the guilt altogether, but if you can't, don't let it inhibit a free exchange of thoughts and feelings about what is going on. Staying grounded in your relationship will enhance your ability to deal with whatever comes up for you with your parent.

So, I have taken care of my aging parents even though I was not prepared to do it. I'm not sure I've done a very graceful job of it, but I share this personal account because I know others have had, are having, or will have a similar experience. We have to allow ourselves the luxury of openly expressing our frustrations about the real impositions on our lives as well as the child-in-the-adult fears that get triggered by such a reversal of roles.

THE NEEDS OF GROWING CHILDREN

If you have children, their evolving needs as they grow may influence how you live your gay or lesbian life. Hopefully, you have enabled your children to deal honestly with who you are and what your relationship is all about. But there may come a time in a child's life when a new level of conflict arises about your being gay. Most likely that will be with the onset of adolescence, when sexuality and identity issues collide and peer approval is critically important.

I would never suggest going back into the closet, but it may be necessary to tone down activities that necessitate public visibility as a gay person, at least temporarily. I have known a number of couples whose children had nothing to say about their parents' gay activism until those children became teenagers. Then came the request to please not be *visible* activists anymore.

Fortunately, the trend seems to be that once adolescence is past the young adult loses the embarrassment about having gay activist parents. I remember two cases when teenage children rebelled against their parents' visibility in the gay movement and then, a few years later, appeared on television to talk about how proud they were that their gay parents were who they were.

Children bring the outside world into the home in ways that create new challenges for the same-sex couple. You may have resolved your coming-out issues with family, friends, and coworkers, but children introduce a whole new layer of people to deal with: teachers and school personnel, fellow students, neighborhood pals.

Maybe you have done a great job of orienting your children to the nature of your loving relationship, but there can be new coming-out dilemmas to be dealt with, and they will probably change in nature with the years. As long as you're all talking about it you will have the information you need to know in order to choose which direction to head in at any one time. Respecting a child's need to manage disclosure while keeping everybody reasonably honest is a task for the wisest of gay and lesbian parents, but I am assuming that is what you are anyway.

THE REST OF THE WORLD

The outside influences in the life of any given gay or lesbian couple are many and varied. What is going on in a particular city, or our country, or the world can be very affecting, especially when gay issues are involved. Our status gets better, it gets worse—we win elections, defeat antigay amendments, triumph in the courts, and we get bashed by self-serving politicians courting the support of the religious right. We lose a battle for antidiscrimination legislation in our own state but gain positive recognition for our issues in the national media.

It's all about keeping a perspective on the progress we as a community have made and will continue to make. It's about the way you as a couple maintain the integrity of your loving relationship, no matter what other demands are made on your life. It's about staying in touch with that center.

CHAPTER 10

Couple Counseling—How Can It Help?

I don't want this to read like a commercial for couple counseling, but, in a sense, that's what it is. I do believe there are times in the lives of some couples when the assistance of a professional counselor can be invaluable, but many people have resistance to seeking such help. They have to be "sold" on the idea.

Counseling or therapy? I am going to use these terms interchangeably, though there are those who would distinguish between the two based on years of education and depth of training. The distinction is a real one. But you may find, at any given time, your sessions with a therapist may focus mainly on the everyday problems of your life and those with a counselor may get more deeply into the dynamics of your personal history. I am simply going to alternate between the two terms *counselor* and *therapist*.

When couples do come to counseling they come in varying stages of readiness to work on their problems. Sometimes both are ready, sometimes one partner wants to get down to work and the other wants only to get out of the room or out of the relationship. Also, there are those who are attuned to the process of therapy, others think it's a waste of time or merely punishment for their misdeeds.

The ability of an individual to cope effectively with crises in life can differ greatly from person to person. Some therapy is mainly about teaching coping skills. In other instances, understanding cause and effect and putting problems in perspective may be the primary focus. When a couple is stuck it is easy to get into the mind-set that this is the way it's always going to be, therefore there's no hope for change or relief.

Coming to understand that everything happens for a reason and that it is possible to identify and change patterns of behavior is a crucial part of any kind of therapy. With couples this is especially important because we too often tend to think that relationship problems are a function of our partner's mental aberrations or evil intent, nothing to do with patterns, or with our own behavior.

WHY DO COUPLES COME TO THERAPY?

The reasons people present for seeking therapy are many and varied.

- A relationship has gone stale; partners have grown apart.
- A couple has become antagonistic but the reason is not apparent.
- One partner has changed in some significant way and

this is seen by the other as a betrayal of their original understanding of one another.
- The couple is having the same fight over and over and can't get to the bottom of it or move on from it.
- Communication has become blocked by some unresolved conflict.
- Sexual issues feel irresolvable.
- External pressures—career, families, children—have become overwhelming to one or both partners.
- Internal pressures—anxiety, depression, anger—have caused one partner to become isolated from the other.
- A traumatic occurrence involving one or both partners has produced continuing tension.

These are just some of the reasons couples present for seeking professional help. Not uncommon to hear in the first session are also such things as:

"We're not in love anymore."
"We fight all the time and we can't stand it."
"I just can't get past the affair to be able to trust again."

While the *presenting* problem may not be the real underlying issue the couple needs to work on, that is what the therapy usually starts with.

RELATIONSHIP GONE STALE

Here are two people who feel bored, flat, without enthusiasm for their life together. Perhaps the relationship has become too routinized, too predictable, there's nothing to look forward to but more of the same. It's comfortable and safe, but where is the excitement of years gone by? Is this all there is?

In counseling there is an opportunity to explore how

and why the excitement isn't there. Is it possible that the next step in the evolution of the couple's intimacy is somehow too daunting to take, involving too many unknowns, presenting too much of a challenge? Or is something being avoided, something unsaid for fear of hurting or losing a partner? Is it safer to keep the lid on?

Melinda and Joan

Melinda and Joan came to therapy because they felt bored with their life together. In the five years of their relationship they had become so entwined they felt sufficient unto one another. They saw fewer people and did fewer things outside the home than they ever had, preferring each other's company to everyone else's. Their life had become routinized and predictable, no surprises, no unexpected turns in the road.

In their sessions Melinda and Joan lamented how unstimulated they felt, loving one another but unmotivated to express that love in any way that would create vulnerability or ask too much of the other person.

I asked the two women to explore what their life would be like if they didn't feel bored. At first they couldn't get beyond their complaints, but eventually they were able to agree that it would be exciting to have a renewed intensity of emotion. When asked how they felt about that, both said the idea was attractive but scary. Neither was sure she could manage opening up that much.

I encouraged the women to speak individually about fears related to intimacy. One spoke of losing the security of an unchallenging emotional life. The other described the anxiety she felt when she thought something was being asked of her that she couldn't deliver. As they did this they began to experience their separateness more, to be interested in the different things the other was saying.

They worried that feelings could become as all-consuming as they had been in the beginning of their relationship. What would happen to the well-ordered life they had constructed? As they talked through their fear of the unknown, of the possible effects of passion revived, they were able to see that their "boredom" was protective—serving to ward off the challenges of greater closeness.

Melinda and Joan worked on being more trusting of themselves and their relationship. Slowly, tentatively, each began to reach out to the other, first verbally, then physically. Having fought back the fears of vulnerability and of the inability to meet expectations, they were more able to venture into the new territory of a growing intimacy.

ANTAGONISM UNEXPLAINED

Nobody knows what is going on, but the relationship is not working. It has grown acrimonious. Anything can set off an argument. Anger erupts sometimes for no reason at all, or so it seems. It is as if something is brewing under the surface of the couple's life, but the partners appear unable to fathom what it is. They try to talk but antagonism takes over.

In the therapist they have someone who can help them explore what is going on in the underground of their relationship—what seems to trigger the antagonism, what purpose it is serving in the relationship. Again, what would their life be like without the acrimony? What is the real source of their anger?

CHANGE AS BETRAYAL

For some people it is as though an unspoken promise was made at the outset of the relationship: "This is who I am and this is who I will always be." Over time people change. Adjustments must be made, but in this relationship one partner is not prepared for the change, doesn't like it, doesn't want it, considers it a betrayal. Even if the change is a rational one—"I just want to have some time to myself"—the other person may feel rejected and abandoned.

The counselor can help to put change in perspective, to facilitate an understanding of what the changes really mean. Wherein lies the threat? Is the objecting partner afraid of losing a lover? Does the lover's changing mean that he or she must make unwanted changes also?

Larry and Sam

Larry and Sam had lived together for four years when Larry decided he was going to take a sabbatical from his job as an accountant. Larry had enough money saved so that he could continue to contribute to the running of the household as he always had. Sam was a little puzzled about why Larry wanted to quit such a well-paying job, but he went along with Larry's plan.

At first Larry just stayed around the house reading and gardening and going for long walks with their dog, Arnold. Then Larry enrolled in a cooking class taught by the owner of a popular local restaurant. Larry had always liked to cook but he now became obsessed with what he was learning. He wanted to talk food all the time, spent his days trying out recipes, and lobbied Sam to be as interested in this new activity as he was.

Sam did not like what was happening. He wasn't that interested in talking about food, and he was afraid that Larry might want to become a full-time professional cook. Though Larry had not talked about doing this, Sam convinced himself that his fear was well founded. Cooks have long hours. Sam imagined spending a lot of time alone. He worried himself into such a state that he thought the relationship might be in jeopardy.

Sam let Larry know that he was unhappy, and he requested that they get some help together. Though Larry didn't quite understand what Sam was so upset about he did agree to enter couple counseling since it seemed so important to his lover.

In therapy Sam talked about his distress at the changes in Larry. He accused Larry of not caring about him or their life together, of being so caught up with his fantasy of being a cook that their relationship no longer mattered to him. Larry was shocked at the intensity of Sam's feelings and at the suggestion that he might become a professional cook, which he had no intention of doing.

As they talked over what was happening it soon became clear that Sam had fears about his ability to hold on to Larry as a lover. It came out that Sam was afraid he was not interesting enough as a person for Larry to want to continue the relationship. These were feelings that Sam had been living with for a long time. Larry's interest in cooking, an activity he pursued alone, outside the relationship, just reinforced Sam's doubts about himself.

Once all of this was out, Larry was able to reassure Sam that he was devoted to him and that his interest in cooking did not signal disillusionment with his lover. Larry was helped to see what Sam needed from him— more explicit expressions of his love and commitment.

Sam came to understand that his insecurity about

himself had affected his ability to rationally assess what was going on in his relationship. He was eventually able to accept Larry's interest in cooking for what it was, a benign change in personal interest that was not a threat to the future of the partnership.

HAVING THE SAME FIGHT OVER AND OVER

This couple comes to therapy to try to stop the merry-go-round they are on. They are tired of the same old argument they so often end up in, no variation, no resolution, no resistance to the compulsion to get into it again and again.

The counselor can help the partners to see what they might be avoiding by staying on such familiar ground. What are the underlying issues that could be too dicey to deal with directly, that the same old argument enables them to not deal with? In *Permanent Partners* I have described such repetitive arguments as the "theater of the relationship," the discussion that is always available as a kind of stage on which to play out a harmless superficial rendering of the real underlying drama.

COMMUNICATION PROBLEMS

Much of what a relationship is about comes down to communication. This couple comes to counseling because one or both feel unheard when it comes to dealing with anything problematical. They attribute to one another a certain intent:

"She only wants to be right. She doesn't care what I'm feeling."

"He is only interested in blaming. He never wants to look at the real truth about himself."

As long as they both stick to their assumptions about the other person, communication is at an impasse. The counselor helps them break through the impasse by enabling them to check out their assumptions, to listen without having to defend against what they might hear, to accept that each partner contributes to every transaction gone wrong. The counselor may then do some educating as to the difference between communication that enhances a relationship and that which inhibits its growth.

Sandy and Jean

Sandy and Jean were in the third year of their relationship and into their first major crisis following a disagreement about whether or not to include Sandy's ex-lover in a group traveling to a women's music festival. Each was angry for different reasons. They came into their first therapy session with guns blazing.

Both were certain that the other person cared only about what she wanted and was failing to be reasonable. The more they talked about it the more agitated they became, each assuming that the other only wanted to win and didn't care what feelings might be hurt in the process. They were locked in an adversarial tug-of-war.

Neither woman appeared able to see the other's point of view. The therapy focused on how they were communicating about the problem they had. As long as both were certain about the other's misguided motives, neither could give up the feeling that she was the one who was right.

In therapy they were encouraged not only to talk about their own feelings but also to be in the shoes of the other, to understand the needs being expressed by their lover's behavior. The lack of an empathic response was one reason they had such anger toward one another.

The therapist pushed for a willingness from each to open up to the other, to communicate feelings, needs, thoughts, and wishes for change directly. When they were both able to do this it became possible to speak without defensiveness, to talk about the deep-down concerns underlying their disagreement. There was no right and wrong, only the conflicting needs of two people who had to clear their communication sufficiently to find a collaborative solution.

SEXUAL ISSUES

There is a sexual issue that feels irresolvable. The couple's previous arrangement about sexual exclusivity may be in question with one or both partners. Perhaps the conflict is about whether to continue having safer sex: one may feel it's necessary; the other that it is no longer necessary. It may be that sex has stopped. Neither partner knows why but both are unhappy about it.

EXTERNAL PRESSURES

In a perfect world the outside demands on two people in a partnership would be the same, equal, and balanced. In our imperfect world *one* partner might possibly have compelling pressures to deal with that affect the quality of the relationship. Families of origin can be particularly demanding or disruptive. Children may be in conflict about a gay or lesbian parent's relationship or activist involvement.

The couple who comes to therapy because external pressures have become too much to handle on their own

will need help in sorting out their priorities and negotiating changes designed to take everyone's needs into
account. The counselor elicits feelings about what is happening and may have to help the partners improve their
negotiating skills.

INTERNAL PRESSURES

Depression, anxiety, and anger are very real to the
person experiencing them, but a partner may have difficulty understanding why someone can't just "get over"
such debilitating feelings. The couple may be at an impasse, the troubled partner feeling trivialized and misunderstood, the impatient partner feeling frustrated and
unheard.

The counselor can help to bring the depressed, anxious, or angry person more into focus—that is, the counselor may encourage the expression of these feelings in
such a way that the other partner has a better grasp of
what it's like to be having this kind of experience. The
counselor might also do a kind of "empathy training,"
helping partner number two learn to tune in to the feelings of the other more readily.

Mark and Danny

Mark had always been a pretty levelheaded guy,
which is why Danny was surprised when Mark seemed to
get totally lost in grieving over his father's death. Mark
and his father, John, had had a civilized relationship,
though it was apparent to all that Mark's father was uncomfortable with his son's being gay. Nevertheless, John
was polite to Mark's lover and never did anything overtly
to put down their relationship.

It had been six months since John's fatal heart attack. Mark had arranged his father's funeral, been comforting to his mother, and handled the estate, for which he was executor. Since Mark was an attorney, his brothers and sisters were all in agreement that he should indeed have been the one put in charge of probate matters.

Danny couldn't have been more supportive of Mark following John's death. When Mark needed to talk about his father, Danny was right there, as he was if Mark felt sad and needed a shoulder to cry on. All the cues were present for what to do, and Danny responded to them. Danny assumed that Mark's grief would abate after a while and their life would get back to normal, but that was not what was happening.

Instead of leveling out, Mark's grief seemed to have taken him over. He was depressed to the point of being silent much of the time. He seemed to have lost interest in socializing, and except for going to work each day, he stayed at home, his main activity lying on the couch with his eyes closed.

Clearly, it was getting worse, not better. Danny tried to ask Mark what was happening but Mark said he didn't know, he just felt terrible about his father's death and he couldn't shake the sadness. Danny didn't know what to do.

After several more months of this Danny become impatient with Mark. He told him that he was being immature, that his life was not affected that much by his father's dying, that his relentless grieving was not normal, and that he should get over himself. Mark just withdrew further.

Danny's impatience grew until he was feeling that he couldn't stand living with so much gloom. He didn't know why Mark was letting this continue and doing nothing to fix it. Danny was at his wits' end. It was at this point that a close friend suggested therapy.

In the therapist's office Danny poured out his feelings but Mark remained silent. Danny was exasperated. After a couple of sessions like this the therapist gently encouraged Mark to talk about his father's death. Mark was hesitant at first but slowly began to say how he felt. He was angry with his father for not being more understanding of him, and he felt guilty for his angry feelings.

As Mark talked more about his feelings it became apparent that he was trapped by contradictory emotions—the sadness of his father's leaving him and the anger he had never expressed while his father was alive. Mark talked about how he felt immobilized by the anger. There was nowhere to go with it. It made him feel guilty. The way he was compensating for the guilt was to lose himself in the grief.

The therapist helped Mark talk in depth about what he was going through. Soon Danny could see that Mark's bereavement was not something he could just "get over." It was more complicated than that. As Danny understood more about what Mark was experiencing, his frustration abated and he began to feel compassionate.

Mark was no longer the recalcitrant partner refusing to give up his grief. He was someone caught in an understandable dilemma. Mark was able to tell Danny how lonely and isolated he'd felt during this period, how alienated he was by Danny's impatient badgering to "get over it." Mark said he'd been unable to talk to Danny at first because he felt ashamed of his feelings, and later because of Danny's attitude.

With the therapist's help Mark worked through the anger that he felt toward his father. Talking out loud about the feelings he'd been dealing with only in his head helped a lot. The process was freeing to Mark, enough so that he could be available once again to his partner and the relationship.

A Traumatic Occurrence

For some couples a serious loss can mean a break in their ability to trust and be supportive of one another, especially if the loss is seen as an avoidable one. It is natural, though not very productive, to place blame. When this happens, the weight of guilt or resentment may be too much for the couple to deal with alone.

The counselor can help the couple get out the unspoken feelings that are creating tension between them. Work can then be done to put the event in perspective, taking into account the whole of the couple's life together. The counselor may be the catalyst for the renewal of trust and support between the partners so that they can contribute to one another's healing.

These are some of the more common reasons couples seek counseling. Again, what the couple ends up working on may be different from what is presented at the outset. While couples' therapy may involve some problem solving, the primary process is one of exploring feelings and facilitating their expression, improving communication, and learning to deal with conflict productively.

WHAT THE THERAPIST CAN DO FOR YOU

At various times, the therapist may serve the couple as a listener, a good parent, an educator, a catalyst, or a guide.

THE THERAPIST AS LISTENER

When you are in conflict with your partner, it can be difficult for you to hear what he or she is saying. There is noise in the system. Preoccupied with your own thoughts and feelings, you may not be able, or want, to let in the information your partner is offering. You are listening to yourself more than to the other person—telling yourself how angry you are, how hurt, how frustrated; wondering what you are doing with this maddening person; wishing you were somewhere else.

The therapist, however, can listen without distraction, free to hear what is truly being said. The value of this is twofold. The therapist is able to hear and clarify messages from one partner to the other, and in so doing models *active* listening.

Sally and Marta

Sally and Marta came to counseling because Sally felt that Marta had become critical and disapproving. She couldn't understand why Marta was angry with her so often. Marta said she didn't feel critical or disapproving, and usually when Sally accused her of being angry, she wasn't.

Week after week the two women brought stories of their disagreements to therapy. Sally invariably accused Marta of being angry with her. Marta consistently said that she had not been angry, but she *was* getting annoyed at having to prove herself all the time.

Then Sally dropped a bombshell. They were discussing an episode of the previous evening when once again Sally felt that she was on the receiving end of Marta's disapproval. Sally said that she felt Marta's unhappiness with her so strongly that she had almost asked if Marta wanted her to move out.

Marta was stunned. Move out? She thought their relationship was solidly established. She had no idea that Sally felt so alienated. Perplexed, Marta implored Sally to tell her what the problem was. Sally said she *had* been telling Marta what the problem was for weeks. It was back to the anger and disapproval that Marta said she had not felt. What was going on?

The therapist, listening *through* their controversy, heard from Sally a plea for support and reassurance. Sally needed to *hear* from Marta that she really did love and approve of her. The problem was not really that Marta was critical and angry, it was that she was not giving Sally the verbal support and reassurance that she needed.

As the therapy progressed, Sally was enabled to tell Marta what she needed from her. Marta, no longer primed to defend herself against another unjust accusation, was able to hear what Sally was saying. The therapist had not only clarified the message but demonstrated that if one *could* listen without defensiveness it was much easier to hear what was really being said.

THE THERAPIST AS GOOD PARENT

Parenting being the daunting challenge it is, many of us have grown up feeling we didn't get our full share of love, support, and guidance from the people who were our parents. We work to remedy this in all kinds of ways, sometimes productively, sometimes disastrously. If there is such a void, the effort to fill it can become a major feature of our close adult relationships.

One positive side effect of the interaction with a therapist is the feeling that here is someone who values you and understands what you need. The therapist doesn't judge, impose his or her own needs on you, or demand compliance with arbitrary rules. The therapist *wants* to know what you are feeling and thinking. Attention is lavished on you in your sessions; you are at the center of the action, just as you may have wished you could be more often with your *real parents*.

This experiencing of the therapist as a good parent can have a corrective emotional effect, especially if your own parent happened to be neglectful, withholding, or abusive. The therapist, parentlike, supplies the caring, support, and attention of a loving, nurturing mother or father. An added benefit may be the validation the therapist/parent gives to your gay or lesbian relationship, something you may or may not get from your own family.

Perhaps you are lucky enough to have parents who do accept and affirm your gay life with your partner, but in those instances where you are not so lucky, a therapist who understands and cares about your life with your partner, and wants to help you improve it, can be a powerful ally when you most need one.

THE THERAPIST AS EDUCATOR

Therapy is always in some way a learning situation. You are learning what's possible for your relationship and your life. You are learning how to separate the past from the present, how to fight constructively, how to communicate and negotiate effectively, how to be more empathic, how to cope with feelings that may seem overwhelming.

The therapist teaches these "skills" in relation to the issues you are struggling with. The teaching may be indirect and subtle or it may be direct and didactic. Some therapists see their role as one of teaching the lessons of life. Others do their educating by allowing you to explore until you find your own answers.

As a lesbian therapist working with gay and lesbian people, I find myself at times educating about what it means to be gay, how to deal with homophobic encounters, what the gay and lesbian community has to offer, how often same-sex relationships work and endure, and why they do.

I become instructive when asked about safer sex, how to manage disclosure to families, or what to consider regarding monogamy versus nonmonogamy. I see these educational tasks as an important part of the role of every therapist to gay and lesbian people. In a sense, we stand in loco parentis to those in our community who are just coming out or who are struggling at any level with who they are as gay or lesbian people.

THE THERAPIST AS CATALYST

An important aspect of couple counseling is the opportunity partners have to ventilate their feelings and tell their side of the story. But more than that has to happen. From the jumble of conflicting accounts of events and interpretations of behavior the therapist must coax out the repetitive patterns that reveal what is really at the heart of the couple's problems.

The therapist, in other words, enables the partners to look at their behavior in a decipherable way. What typically causes conflict? At what point does dialogue break down? What brings relief? The therapist enables discussion of what each partner wants to be different—what changes are necessary to bring harmony back to the partnership.

Sometimes the therapist facilitates confrontation

when clients are unable to tell one another what they honestly feel. Partners may be afraid to take a chance on the consequences of confrontation, or they may not have learned the language of emotions sufficiently to be able to communicate what they feel inside.

The therapist can be a catalyst in the modeling of responsiveness, *particularly* with clients who tend not to show their emotions. One partner opens up and pours out feelings about something and the other just sits there impassively as though nothing had been said. The therapist may then, in a sense, *loan* his or her emotions to the client.

"Ouch! That hurts. John, how does it feel hear Joe say those things to you?"

This has the potential not only of modeling behavior but of giving permission to express feelings that may have become taboo in the relationship. This is especially true when one or both partners threaten flight as a way of saying they are dissatisfied with something. The culture of the relationship then becomes one of inhibited communication—swallow your feelings if you want to keep your lover.

The therapist highlights the subversiveness of threatening dissolution. Fear of losing your partner hardly encourages open and honest interaction. Inhibited communication is the enemy of intimacy. The therapist as catalyst pushes through the barriers created by threats of abandonment and the protective silence that often ensues.

THE THERAPIST AS GUIDE

While dealing with emerging problems and patterns in the couple's life is necessary to progress in therapy, a next step is the exploration of choices and options for the future. Here the counselor is a guide helping clients integrate the information and insights acquired so far. The therapist as guide helps move the process forward in such a way as to maximize hope for the future—change is possible as long as two people are willing and able to talk about what they want.

WHAT THE COUPLE BRINGS

TO THE THERAPY

While most therapists would like to think of themselves as powerful agents of change, the fact is that the effectiveness of the therapy is largely determined by the clients. If one of the partners has been dragged reluctantly into the situation, it is likely that not much progress will be made until that person decides there is something in it for her or him.

How close are one or both partners to giving up? Is the therapy a gesture—one last effort to kick-start the relationship and do it in a hurry, or forget it? There is probably not a good prognosis for this couple unless they are willing to give counseling a reasonable period of time to work.

Then there are those who are certain that *everything* wrong in the relationship is the fault of the other person. Preliminary work here has to address this appealing but quite misguided notion. Relationship problems are never the sole product of one person's behavior.

The couple's level of commitment to one another is the foundation on which continuity and closeness are built. If both partners are truly committed to improving their life together the chances are very good that they will be able to use the therapy to do that.

When one partner is unsure about what he or she wants, that indecision will influence the course of the counseling. One of the first orders of business will be to look at why the indecision exists—what is, or is not, happening in the relationship that causes the person to have doubts about its future.

Michael and Joe

Michael and Joe had been together for twelve years, when Michael, out of the blue, told Joe that he was thinking about ending the relationship. Joe was thrown off balance. He hadn't been aware that anything was wrong, certainly not *that* wrong. In their efforts to talk about what was happening, the discussions didn't seem to go anywhere, and Joe was left as perplexed as he had been before they talked. He couldn't understand why this was happening after twelve years.

Responding to Joe's distress, Michael agreed to postpone his decision and go to couple counseling. In the sessions, there was much discussion of the disagreements they'd had, those sticking points that led to so much unresolved conflict. Joe kept repeating that he didn't see any of that as a reason to give up an investment of twelve years. Michael remained silent.

They seemed to be getting nowhere until the therapist asked Michael to focus on how he saw his life without Joe. What would he be doing that he couldn't do now? How would his life be different? The floodgates opened and Michael poured out his dissatisfactions with Joe as a partner. He was frustrated with Joe's lack of ambition and his passivity in the face of conflict.

Michael wanted a partner who had a career he was excited about. He wanted someone he could spar with,

who would give as good as he got. Michael did not see
Joe as that person. Joe didn't talk about his work at all,
and when they had a conflict Joe would walk away from
it, saying that they shouldn't fight because it was too
disruptive.

Michael said he had not spoken of this before because he didn't want to hurt Joe's feelings, but he had
been sitting with this dissatisfaction for years. Joe looked
at Michael incredulously. He said he didn't talk about
his work because he didn't think Michael was interested.
And fighting was unpleasant to him, but if that was what
was needed to keep the relationship going he was ready
for round one.

Though it seemed like an overnight transformation,
Joe made good on his word. It was as if the information
from Michael had cleared the air for him. He began to
talk about his career and to seek an advancement he had
thought about for a long time. When he and Michael
got into a conflict Joe took the initiative in putting the issue on the table and saying how he felt about it. He
stood his ground, staying engaged until some resolution
was reached.

With these changes, Michael's feelings about the future of the partnership shifted. No longer interested in
leaving, Michael became invested in renewing the bond
with his lover. The relationship took on a texture it
hadn't had before.

Some therapists who do couple counseling say they
are mainly treating the relationship rather than the
people in it, but it is the difficulty the people in the relationship have in dealing with the frustrations of their
lives that has brought them to therapy in the first place.
Sometimes the therapy has to be about just that

frustration—learning to cope with anger and hurt and disappointment and still be able to trust and love.

The quality of the therapeutic experience will also be very much influenced by the expectations clients bring to the process. This is especially true in couple counseling, where there may be *two* sets of expectations that involve competing agendas. Partner number one may want it finally defined that he or she is the victim of the other person's villainy. Partner number two may want only the opportunity to convince the other to cherish and continue the relationship. The therapist has to keep it all clear and help the couple end up with one shared goal for their partnership.

All of these elements brought to the therapy by the clients will either enhance or slow the rate of progress. In the best-case scenario, two people come to counseling committed to helping their relationship thrive, with their reasons for being there in sync, ready to work diligently on whatever issues come to the surface.

SOME OF THE PRACTICAL ASPECTS OF
SEEKING AND BEING IN THERAPY

Once you decide to seek therapy there are often questions. Does it matter if you see a gay or a nongay therapist? Where does one look to find a qualified person? Should you see the counselor as a couple only or also individually? If you are already in individual therapy should there be coordination of the couple counselor with your personal therapist? How do you know when it's time to stop therapy?

GAY VERSUS NONGAY

Much depends on where you live. If you live in an urban center, I recommend seeing one of the many qualified openly gay or lesbian therapists you'll find there. Why? I believe it is valuable to consult a person who understands from personal experience what it means to grow up gay or lesbian. If the person is openly gay, it means he or she has come to terms with his or her sexuality and can be an example of how freeing a positive gay identity can be.

There may also be information about the gay and lesbian community that is relevant to what you have to work on. With a gay therapist there is usually no need to educate as to what you are talking about. He or she probably knows the references, the places, the events, the developments, and even the people in the community you are talking about.

While a nongay therapist may be totally supportive of your relationship, the gay therapist will have been there, dealing on a personal level with the issues unique to same-sex partnerships. That knowledge can impart a depth of understanding that the nongay counselor is unlikely to have.

But what if you don't live in an urban center with an evolved gay and lesbian community? What if there is no choice about gay or nongay? Then you must either travel to the nearest city or do some careful research to find a local nongay counselor who is accepting and understanding of gay relationships. How do you find that out? You can interview potential therapists on the phone, asking directly about their experience working with gay or lesbian couples.

If you cannot find a nongay counselor who feels okay to you, some gay and lesbian therapists in the larger

cities will do telephone therapy. Calling the gay and lesbian community center in the largest city nearby is a way
to get the names of qualified therapists who might be
available to do phone therapy.

HOW TO FIND A COUNSELOR

The best way to connect with a therapist you'll like is
through referral from a friend who has had a good experience with that person. Ask around. If no such referral
is available, you will have to do the research on your
own. First, you must consider whether you can afford
private therapy. If not, there are clinics and counseling
centers available in most cities and towns. Often they are
affiliated with a university or local hospital.

If you are exploring a clinic setting, you should ask
the intake worker if there is a gay or lesbian counselor
on staff. If the answer is no, ask if there is anyone who
has had experience working with same-sex couples. You
may not get a satisfactory response, but if you don't ask
you'll never know.

In the larger cities you will have gay social service organizations (usually listed in the white pages) to consult
for referrals. Also, there will be ads in gay and lesbian
publications, bulletin boards in bookstores and coffee-
houses, and gay hot lines and switchboards. One national publication, the *Gayellow Pages*, lists therapists and
clinics in various cities. It can be found in most gay or
feminist bookstores.

I suggest interviewing potential counselors in the
first phone contact, saying a bit about your situation. Often you can tell from this initial contact if the person
sounds like someone you would like to talk to.

I will forgo getting heavily into the various disciplines
and schools of therapy available. But, as you probably

know, psychiatrists are M.D.'s who specialize in mental health issues. Clinical psychologists cannot prescribe medications (that may change), but they can usually do almost everything else a psychiatrist can do.

Social workers are psychotherapists if they have a clinical education. In California, there are many marriage and family counselors (MFCs) who are trained and qualified and usually charge less than the psychiatrists, psychologists, or social workers. In other states there are equivalents of MFCs, often called something similar.

Theoretical orientation is not as important here as a sophistication about relationships and an affirmative attitude toward gays and lesbians. There are therapists who will focus mainly on the present and changing behavior. Others will want to make connections to past history. Still others will look at the relationship as a system to be treated in terms of the interaction of its working parts.

INDIVIDUALLY OR TOGETHER?

In the main, couple counseling should involve both partners. Some therapists will never see the partners individually. I do at times have individual sessions alternating or replacing joint sessions when I think it would be useful to the couple. I do not do it routinely. Some therapists do. I believe it is very important always to have the other partner's permission when I set up an individual session.

COORDINATING WITH AN INDIVIDUAL THERAPIST

If you are already in individual therapy, it is a good idea to have your personal therapist get in touch with your couple counselor so that they do not find themselves working at cross purposes.

In one instance I was waging an uphill battle to get two

men to work through their problems and continue their commitment to each other. Then I discovered that one partner's individual therapist was encouraging him to feel free to move on from the relationship if he wasn't satisfied. We were certainly working at cross purposes, creating confusion all around. A consultation solved the problem.

PREVENTIVE COUPLE COUNSELING

I want to quote here a friend, psychotherapist Michael Shernoff:

> With increasing frequency I see couples for two or three sessions before they move in together, or around some significant life transition they are considering as a couple such as adopting or having a child, relocating, or one partner stopping work to return to graduate school. These sessions help the couple insure that they have examined a poignant event or transition in their life in an effort to prevent it from becoming a crisis. In addition, the concept of the relationship tune-up every now and then for one or two sessions is another tool to suggest to couples who are seeking ways to help them stay in long-term partnerships.*

HOW DO YOU KNOW WHEN
TO STOP THERAPY?

It's easier to talk about when you should *not* stop therapy. If the going is getting rough and you are uncomfortable with what is coming out in the sessions, talk

*Personal correspondence, May 1995.

about your discomfort; *don't just stop therapy*. If you are just gliding along, and it feels as if you are not making progress, think about what you might be avoiding bringing up. Tell the therapist how you feel about what is happening, but *don't just stop therapy*.

The decision to stop should be a joint one between the couple and the therapist. Most therapists are conscientious about not hanging on to clients past the time they should depart. After reviewing why a couple came to therapy and where they are with regard to those issues, it should be apparent to all when the time comes to call it a day.

I like to have a transitional period when I may see the couple every other week for a while, creating the opportunity for discussing feelings about separating from me and the therapy process. Some couples are ready when the time comes to make a clean break; a couple of weeks is sufficient to wind up. Others feel anxious about terminating and need a longer period of making the transition.

FINALLY . . .

As with any process that is as abstract as counseling, it is sometimes difficult to know if it is something that is for you. I can only tell you that in twenty-five years of working with gay and lesbian couples, I have become convinced that this kind of therapy can be enormously useful when a relationship runs into obstacles. It is a resource for discovery, for healing, and for revitalizing the most important connection in your life.

Epilogue: Stability, Continuity, Renewal, and the Joy of Never Having to Go out on Another Date

ASSUMING PERMANENCE

"You've been together twenty-two years? That is so wonderful!"

I feel heroic. What an accomplishment. I smile proudly. I think of the years of not running away from the hard issues, of wanting to flee at times but sticking it out, of forming and re-forming the relationship until its contours are a comfortable fit. My partner and I have stretched, made room for differences, negotiated, accommodated, and above all, assumed permanence. The reward is stability and continuity.

<u>STABILITY</u>

I had been single through most of my adult years, free to come and go, private and independent, very much the master of my own fate. Then I met Terry and we became lovers. It was wonderful, just what I had been dreaming of, an attachment that made me feel loved and appreciated. I mattered more than ever before because I mattered so much to her.

One day Terry proposed that we get serious about being a couple, that we live together and share our lives. The rosy glow faded and was replaced by a rush of terror. I had never committed myself completely to anyone before. I wasn't sure what it even meant. It just felt dangerous.

I was surprised at the level of anxiety her proposal had induced. I pictured my life becoming destabilized, freedom lost, control relinquished, constraints on my individuality. Would I be co-opted by the demands of such a relationship? Would I be up to meeting those demands?

My fears were mainly organized around the threat of loss. I didn't realize at the time what a tenuous hold I must have had on the sense that I could control my life. The threat of another person's moving into my sphere of being, and remaining there, was almost overwhelming.

I struggled with these feelings, trying desperately to get it all right side up again. It was a while before I could work through the fears and come to a decision based on the positive aspects of our experience together. I took the plunge, and we were joined in holy real estate.

I did not become destabilized, quite the opposite. I found a new level of confidence in my dealings with the world, knowing that there was someone who cared

enough to build her life around me. No longer preoccupied with who I would see next and what I would do on
the weekend, I was freer to pursue interests I had put
aside—I felt *more* in control of my time and energy.

I soon came to see that it wasn't individuality that was
lost, it was an added component to my identity that was
gained. Individuality isn't the freedom to reinvent yourself every day, it is about the sense of who you are separate from all the other people around you, including
your lover.

I had a positive sense of myself that got reinforced every time I was in my partner's presence. I actually got
myself into better focus than I ever had before. Instead
of looking into many mirrors searching for an image
that I could feel good about, I had one marvelously
bright, clear reflection of myself that told me I was desirable and loved.

I came to realize that the commitment two people
make to one another becomes the base of strength from
which they meet the challenges of their individual lives.
That is the essence of stability in relationship and the
key to how a committed partnership can *increase* one's
personal choices.

CONTINUITY

Let's say you are a heterosexual person in a heterosexual family. You have regular contact with your parents
and grandparents. You have children, and they have
regular contact with their grandparents and great-
grandparents. This is generational continuity, and it conveys a sense of being a part of, belonging to, something.

While more gay and lesbian people are having children, they are still in the minority, so that sense of gen-

erational continuity is missing for most of us. It is the blueprint of what was and what will be. We proceed without that, and if we spend much time in serial monogamous relationships the discontinuity is even more apparent.

It is in the enduring permanent partnership that gay and lesbian people have the best chance to create the experience of relationship continuity. We do that through developing with our partner a shared history, traditions and customs unique to our life as a couple, and the expectation that we are going to be together as a family as long as we live.

We make our own blueprint, our own sense of who we are and who we are going to be. We are grounded in the partnership. It becomes our past and our future. We do that in much the same way we make our own blueprint in the gay and lesbian community, defining ourselves from the intrinsic truth of who we are.

Continuity in relationship gives one a sense of belonging that is expressed in the "we" of one's memories and plans.

"Remember when we decided to live together, how excited we both were?"

"Remember when we had such a tiny place we had to sleep on the sofa when guests came?"

"Remember the first time we met each other's families?"

"We are going to have a recommitment ceremony."

"We are planning ways to take care of our parents when the time comes."

"We are thinking of adopting a child."

Continuity shapes how we organize our thinking about our relationship life. In addition to the "we" aspect, a certain amount of mutuality is involved in all our planning and decision making. We attend to markers of our life, such as anniversaries, that inform us of time passing, and common reference points that recall a shared backlog of experiences.

And then there is that final perk of continuity and permanence—the joy of never having to go out on another date. What is so joyous about that? Do I have to tell you? With your permanent partner you don't have to be "on" all the time, to perform and always be on your best behavior. You don't have to be on trial, auditioning for the part of Ms. or Mr. Right, competing with someone's fantasy of the perfect companion. You don't have to worry about that next phone call. You are home free.

RENEWAL

It is in the integration of continuity and renewal that long-term intimate relationships keep their spark alive. Renewal can take many forms. Here are a few: resurrecting the language of love, reawakening the spirit of courtship (without the angst), and renewing commitment to the relationship.

RESURRECTING THE LANGUAGE OF LOVE

In some long-term relationships, partners have mellowed out to a point where they are on emotional cruise control. There is the perfunctory hug at the beginning and the end of the day and that's about it. While emotional neutrality can be comfortable, there may come a time when one or both partners feel something has been lost in their interaction—they sense a detachment that can be mistaken for disinterest.

"What happened to us?" I hear from clients. "Where did the passion go? Are you still attracted to me? Why don't you ever say so?"

What is usually happening is not rejection or disinterest, but inertia.

"Oh, I just got out of the habit of love talk. Why do I have to say it? He [she] knows how I feel."

A relationship that has fallen into silence on the subject of affection needs to be resuscitated. Most people *need* to hear that they are appreciated, admired, attractive, and loved. And they need to hear it from the person closest to them.

Let's assume you are someone in a relationship in which you are not hearing much about yourself—those sweet affirmations that feel so good. You say you've gotten used to it, but every now and then you think how nice it would be to hear from your lover that you look great, are wonderful to be around, and are still the love of her or his life.

I have a little exercise I offer to clients who tell me they are in this kind of situation. It goes like this:

Set aside time with your partner when there are no distractions for a while.

Sit close to each other.

Look into each other's eyes.

Take turns doing these things for about five minutes:

Talk about what you admire most about your partner.

Tell of your appreciation for what your partner has done for you.

Say what is still very attractive to you about him or her.

Speak of the love you feel.

Maintain eye contact while you are talking.

Don't try to control your feelings. Laugh, cry, touch.

If you get stuck and find you can't continue, try to talk about why.

Don't quit. Help each other. Do your best to get the words out.

What I hear most often from clients when I suggest doing this is that it *sounds scary.*

"I'm afraid I won't be able to do it."

"I'm afraid I'll cry."

"I'm afraid of what I'll hear."

"It will bring up feelings I don't want to deal with."

Why is it so difficult to speak of love and admiration and attraction? For some people, talking about these things makes them feel uncomfortably vulnerable.

"I am giving up control," one said.

"This opens me up too much. I'm afraid of that," another said.

Here work must be done on the quality of trust in the relationship. The person with the fears needs to learn that being vulnerable is not giving up all control, it is actually necessary for the relationship to have depth. It works best if both partners are willing and able to allow access to their fragility. That is when trust truly grows.

REAWAKENING THE SPIRIT OF COURTSHIP

So you're two "old married people" now and settled into the routines of your life. You know each other pretty well, and one can usually predict what the other is thinking. Therefore it comes as a big surprise when your partner begins to complain about the lack of excitement in the relationship.

What does this mean, lack of excitement? The two of you have plenty happening—friends, travel, parties, events. What more is needed? Life is quite full. You talk more about it, and eventually you come to understand that what is missing for your lover is the excitement of *courtship*—the new beginnings of love, romantic encounters, and the suspense of not knowing what is going to happen next.

People sometimes hang on to their memories of a period when life seemed like a shining star. They remember the titillation of fantasizing about the person they didn't yet really know. They cherish the discoveries that brought the person into focus like a photograph in a developing tray, the image coming clearer all the time.

Courtship is a time of being adored, seduced, and celebrated, so the person feels very special and wanted. It is like the culmination of a lifetime of dreaming about romance. Your memories are a turn-on, and when you think of it all happening again with *this person*, it is an even greater turn-on.

Okay, you can't turn back the clock, but you can bring back the fun and excitement of romance if you are willing to take the trouble to do something a little different. Here's what several of my clients have done.

One couple plans two nights a month devoted to a fantasy in which they are the major players. Romance is the theme. Sometimes the evening involves an elaborate playing out of the theme with adornments and props. Sometimes it is simple and straightforward, but always the responsibilities and worries of being serious adults disappear for a few hours. They can be silly and sexy and reconnect, newly endeared to each other.

Another couple writes each other love letters once a month, as though they *were* courting again. They read the letters aloud, then add them to their collection—

love notes documenting their affection. Sometimes they pretend they are other people smitten with one another by a chance meeting, writing of their infatuation, proposing libidinous adventures.

They come away from these sessions recharged, intriguing themselves during the month with fresh ideas for their next encounter. It's harmless fun and it boosts their erotic interest in one another.

There are other ways to resurrect the spirit of courtship. The ways I have described may be too contrived for you. You may feel more comfortable with candlelight dinners, soft music, and whatever else temporarily transports you out of the realm of your everyday reality. The point is that a change of pace is revitalizing and can be as important to the health of a relationship as constancy and continuity.

RENEWING COMMITMENT

My lover and I decided we would go all out for our fifteenth anniversary—to recommit our relationship with a ceremony and a black-tie dinner-dance at the Beverly Hills Hotel for a hundred and fifty of our closest friends. The year was 1988.

Was this madness? I wondered. Would this swanky joint really go for a ballroom full of faggots and dykes dancing and hugging and kissing and celebrating ourselves?

We'd been to dozens of gay community fund-raising dinners at large hotels, but we'd never heard of anything *publicly* gay taking place at the posh old pink palace on Sunset Boulevard.

Our adventure began with the hotel catering manager, a woman of a certain age, steely gray eyes, blue hair, *hauteur* personified. Peering at us over gold-rimmed half-glasses, she smiled patronizingly and asked what we would like to arrange.

"A dinner-dance," I said.

She pulled a form out of the top drawer of her desk and wrote.

"And is this event celebrating something?"

"Yes, a fifteenth anniversary."

She wrote.

"And whose anniversary is this?"

"Ours."

She stopped writing, but she didn't look up.

"Yours? The two of you?"

"Yes."

She did look up. We smiled. She nodded, looking off into the middle distance.

"And when would you like to do this?"

"Sometime next month."

She pulled out a calendar and studied it. Finally, she suggested several dates. We picked one. She wrote. She then handed us menus and a price list. We could take them home, make our decisions, and let her know. She would mail us a contract. We said our good-byes and left.

Internalized homophobia lurks everlastingly in the nooks and crannies of the most liberated gay or lesbian brain. I was absolutely certain we would receive not a contract but a letter from the Beverly Hills Hotel saying they were sorry but . . .

I was quite wrong. We received a contract *and* a polite letter saying they were happy to serve us and would look forward to our event. The world was changing. We were changing the world.

I spent the next few weeks in a studio editing a video that told the story of our fifteen-year partnership. We had still photos and film footage of us being at home, giving parties, and doing our gay and lesbian activist turns—marching in parades, doing television interviews, giving speeches. I put it all together with a voice-over narrative and a music track, not Academy Award stuff, but a way to show our guests where our relationship has taken us over the years.

All our friends and members of our families attended the event. Everyone was formally attired, the men (and some of the women) in black tie, a handsome and exuberant crowd. At the end of the cocktail hour, a hush fell over the room as we announced we were going to take our recommitment vows. We read in counterpoint the following:

As light comes to the day
And spring follows the retreat of winter
We illuminate each other's lives
And hold ourselves close for the warmth
That we create together.

We have traveled through many places in our journey
Not always venues to delight
There were the dark meanderings through tunnels
That seemed to have lost their openings
The terrible illusion of no exit
Until reason healed the sight
And there was light at both ends of the tunnel.

We've learned together and taught each other
We've forgotten the lessons and forsaken each other
But the road came around in a circle
And we were joined again, smarter, stronger, and more
    bonded than before.

We know each other now
We've broken all the codes

And seen inside all the Chinese boxes
Inside Chinese boxes inside Chinese boxes.

We are an open book to one another
But we still turn the pages very carefully
Just in case a clue was overlooked, a nuance missed
A theme not fully comprehended.

Now we come before you
Our family who are friends
Our friends who are family
To renew a commitment to our love
We pledge to preserve the integrity of our friendship
As we face each new day rising to seize its promise
    together.

To symbolize our commitment
We exchange these rings
Three intertwining circles to represent
Past, present, and future
To remind us that the past informs the present
And the present shapes the future.

And from this continuity that we experience together
We know with certainty
That our lives are intertwined
Beyond the passing importance of this ritual
To create the bond that is family.

We exchanged our rings and kissed and glowed to
the applause that filled the room. After dinner a lively
and raucous women's band played. Everybody danced,
men with men, women with women, men and women together. Between dances, guests stepped up to an open
microphone and, in a self-indulgence that we thoroughly
enjoyed, paid tribute to us individually and as a couple.
It was a memorable evening, and it was photographed,

videotaped, and reported in the gay press. One such write-up began:

> Marlene Dietrich would not have been out of place, nor would the ghost of Tyrone Power have disturbed the atmosphere by so much as a ripple. That is, not if Power had dragged Errol Flynn from his sepulchral closet and Dietrich had shown up with Garbo on her arm.

Our recommitment at fifteen years remains a cardinal event in our shared history. We did it to rejoice in our union and to mark the passage of our time together. I heartily recommend the experience—whether it's done elaborately, with a cast of hundreds, or simply, with a few friends and family. It is about having our relationships witnessed, honored, and strengthened.

Anniversaries are splendid occasions on which to pay tribute to the viability of these partnerships that are so often trivialized by society. We need to show the world—and not incidentally, the gay and lesbian part of it as well—that couples can have the long life together so many say they want.

Stability and continuity are the cornerstones of a durable relationship tradition. We must strive to achieve that, not only for ourselves but for all gay and lesbian people. We need a cohesive force within our community in order to be as resilient as we must be. Our permanent partnerships, enduring and stable, can be that force, a base of strength from which to meet and change the world.

References

Berzon, Betty. *Permanent Partners: Building Gay and Lesbian Relationships That Last.* New York: Dutton, 1988.

————, ed. *Positively Gay.* Berkeley, Calif.: Celestial Arts, 1992.

Blumstein, Philip, and Pepper Schwartz. *American Couples.* New York: William Morrow, 1983.

Caster, Wendy. *The Lesbian Sex Book.* Boston: Alyson Publications, 1993.

Clunis, D. Merilee, and G. Dorsey Green. *Lesbian Couples.* Seattle, Wash.: Seal Press, 1988.

Cutter, Rebecca. *When Opposites Attract: Right Brain/Left Brain Relationships and How to Make Them Work.* New York: Dutton, 1994.

Fisher, Roger, and Scott Brown. *Getting Together: Building Relationships As We Negotiate.* New York: Penguin Books, 1989.

Gayellow Pages. Renaissance House, Box 292, Village Station, New York, N.Y. 10014.

Island, David, and Patrick Letellier. *Men Who Beat the Men Who Love Them*. New York: Harrington Park Press, 1991.

Jarvik, Lissy, and Gary Small. *Parentcare: A Commonsense Guide for Grown-up Children*. New York: Bantam Books, 1990.

McWhirter, David, and Andrew Mattison. *The Male Couple: How Relationships Develop*. Englewood Cliffs, N.J.: Prentice-Hall, 1984.

Michael, Robert T.; John H. Gagnon; Edward O. Laumann; and Gina Kolata. *Sex in America: A Definitive Study*. Boston: Little, Brown, 1994.

Moore, Thomas. *Soul Mates: Honoring the Mysteries of Love and Relationship*. New York: HarperCollins, 1994.

Renzetti, Claire M. *Violent Betrayal: Partner Abuse in Lesbian Relationships*. Newbury Park, Calif.: Sage Publications, 1992.

Schwartz, Pepper. *Peer Marriages: How Love Between Equals Really Works*. New York: The Free Press, 1994.

Silverstein, Dr. Charles, and Felice Picano. *The New Joy of Gay Sex*. New York: HarperPerennial, 1992.

INDEX

abandonment:
  fear of, 52–53, 88
  feeling of, 80–81; *see also*
    loneliness
abuse, 10, 210–13
  definition of, 211
  help for victims of, 212–13
AIDS, *see* HIV and AIDS
Al-Anon, 216–17
Alcoholics Anonymous (AA), 215,
  217
alcoholism, 139, 214–18
ambivalence zone, 32–33
American Couples (Blumstein and
  Schwartz), 148
anger, 31, 32, 45, 75
  AIDS and, 207–8
  avoidance of conflict and, 182,
    184
  bad kid and, 95, 98
  couple counseling and, 244,
    246, 252, 254, 256, 257
  as irrational, 76, 78, 79, 170
  mean kid and, 104–5
  old, letting go of, 129–34
  parents' emotional legacy and,
    49–51
  scared kid and, 88, 90, 91
  sex and, 139, 157
  see also conflict
anxiety, couple counseling and,
  244, 252
arguing, *see* conflict

bad kid, 8, 87, 94–98, 107
Blumstein, Philip, 148
body-type trap, 150–51
boredom, 7, 63, 73–76

couple counseling and, 243,
  244–46
see also routines
boundaries, 45
  loss of individuality and, 25–29
bridging phrases, 113
Brown, Scott, 119

career, *see* work and career
caregiving, 71
  to ill partner, 203–4, 205–6, 208,
    209
  to parents, 21, 23–24, 235–39
Caster, Wendy, 144
change(s), 10, 191–220
  abuse, *see* abuse
  AIDS and other serious illnesses,
    10, 202–10
  communication and, 192–93
  couple counseling and, 243–44,
    247–49
  external, 193–202
  in income, 197–202
  internal, 191–93
  in job status, 193–97
  in relationship "contracts,"
    218–20
  resistance to, 166
  substance abuse, 10, 213–18
  see also growth
children, 11, 239–40, 272
  couple counseling and, 244, 251
child within, 7–8, 86–108, 168
  bad, 8, 87, 94–98, 107
  balancing adult self with, 8,
    105–8
  mean, 8, 87, 102–5, 107
  needy, 8, 87, 91–94, 106, 168
  scared, 8, 87–91, 107–8